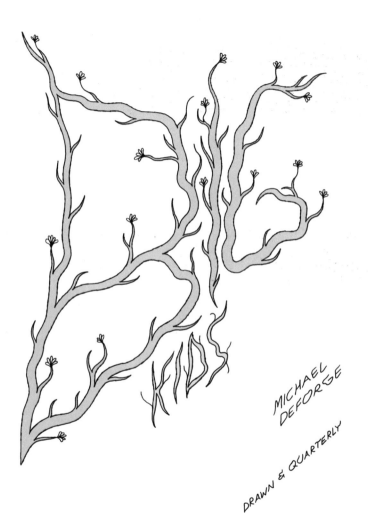

MICHAEL
DEFORGE

DRAWN & QUARTERLY

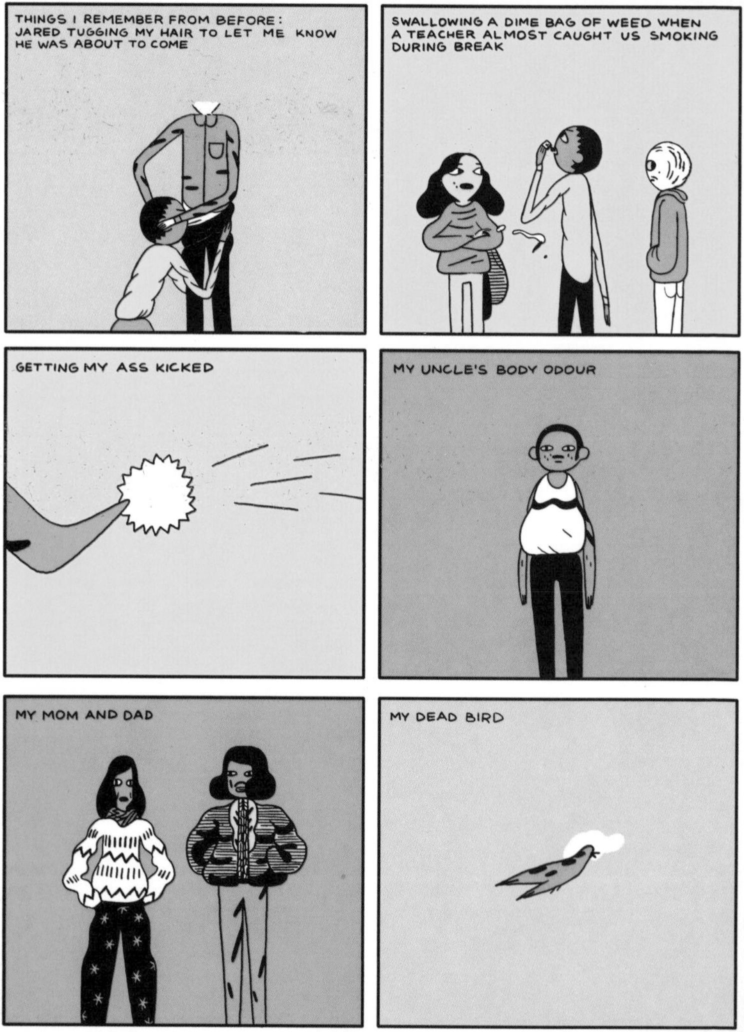
THINGS I REMEMBER FROM BEFORE: JARED TUGGING MY HAIR TO LET ME KNOW HE WAS ABOUT TO COME
SWALLOWING A DIME BAG OF WEED WHEN A TEACHER ALMOST CAUGHT US SMOKING DURING BREAK
GETTING MY ASS KICKED
MY UNCLE'S BODY ODOUR
MY MOM AND DAD
MY DEAD BIRD

MY DEAD BROTHER

THE WAY I LOOKED (OLD HAIR)

USING A BAT ON A STORE WINDOW

DO IT!

WHAT ARE YOU WAITING FOR?!!

LICKING MY COME OFF JARED'S PALM

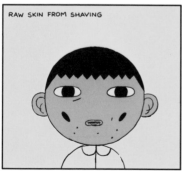

RAW SKIN FROM SHAVING

KIDS TAKING TURNS SPITTING IN MY MOUTH

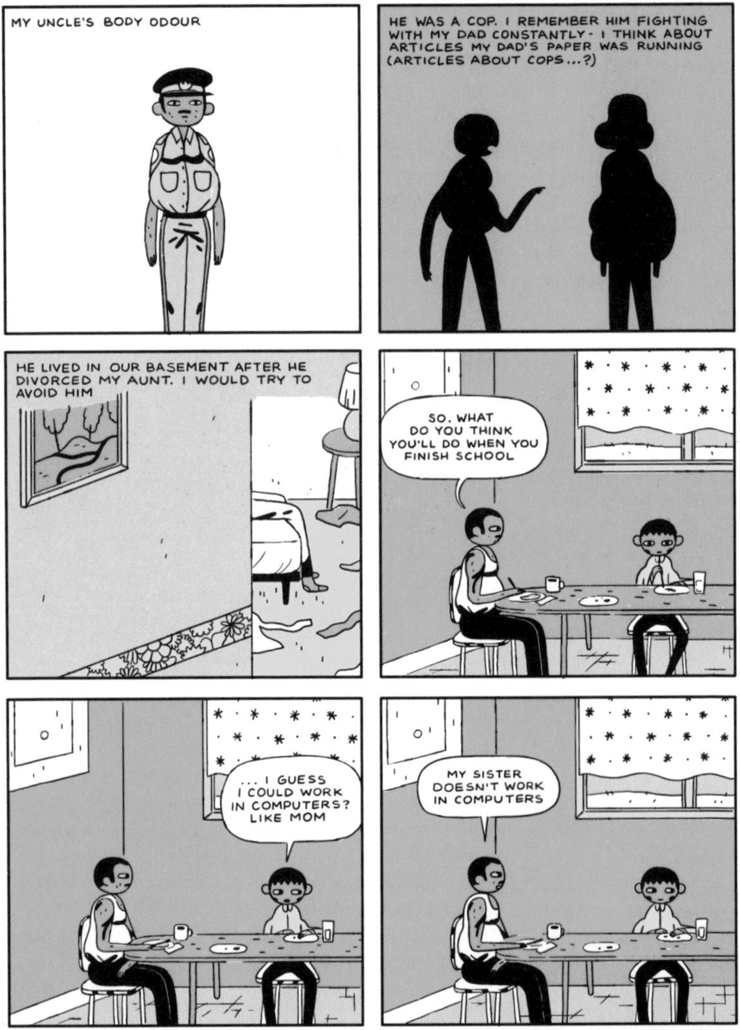
MY UNCLE'S BODY ODOUR
HE WAS A COP. I REMEMBER HIM FIGHTING WITH MY DAD CONSTANTLY - I THINK ABOUT ARTICLES MY DAD'S PAPER WAS RUNNING (ARTICLES ABOUT COPS...?)
HE LIVED IN OUR BASEMENT AFTER HE DIVORCED MY AUNT. I WOULD TRY TO AVOID HIM
SO. WHAT DO YOU THINK YOU'LL DO WHEN YOU FINISH SCHOOL
... I GUESS I COULD WORK IN COMPUTERS? LIKE MOM
MY SISTER DOESN'T WORK IN COMPUTERS

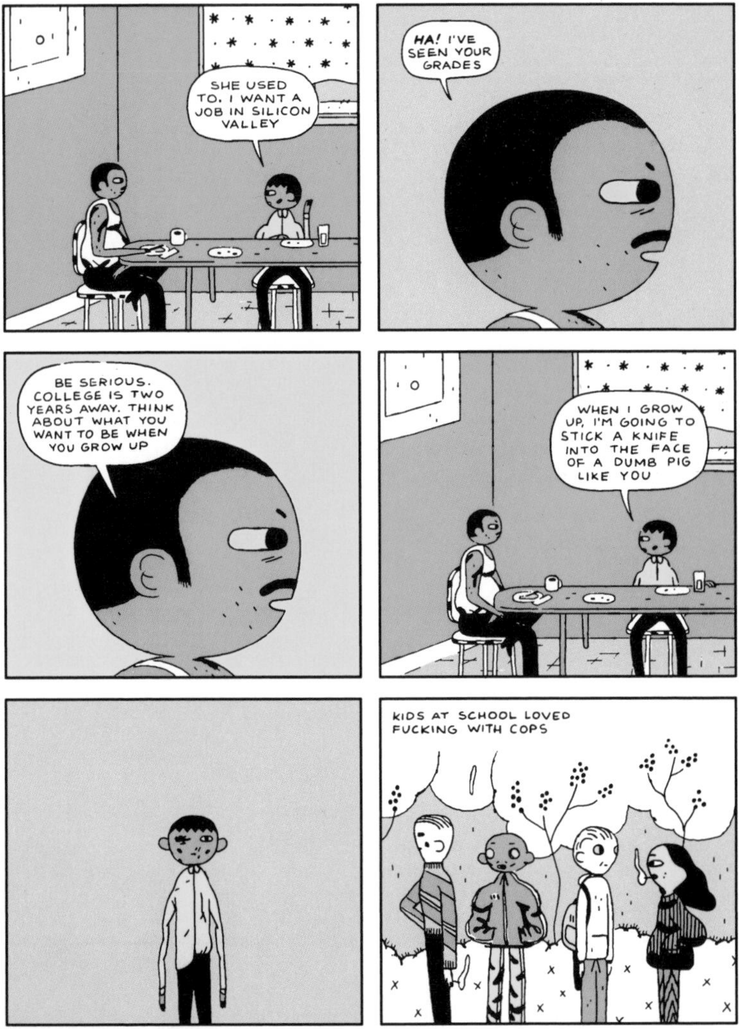
SHE USED TO. I WANT A JOB IN SILICON VALLEY
HA! I'VE SEEN YOUR GRADES
BE SERIOUS. COLLEGE IS TWO YEARS AWAY. THINK ABOUT WHAT YOU WANT TO BE WHEN YOU GROW UP
WHEN I GROW UP, I'M GOING TO STICK A KNIFE INTO THE FACE OF A DUMB PIG LIKE YOU
KIDS AT SCHOOL LOVED FUCKING WITH COPS

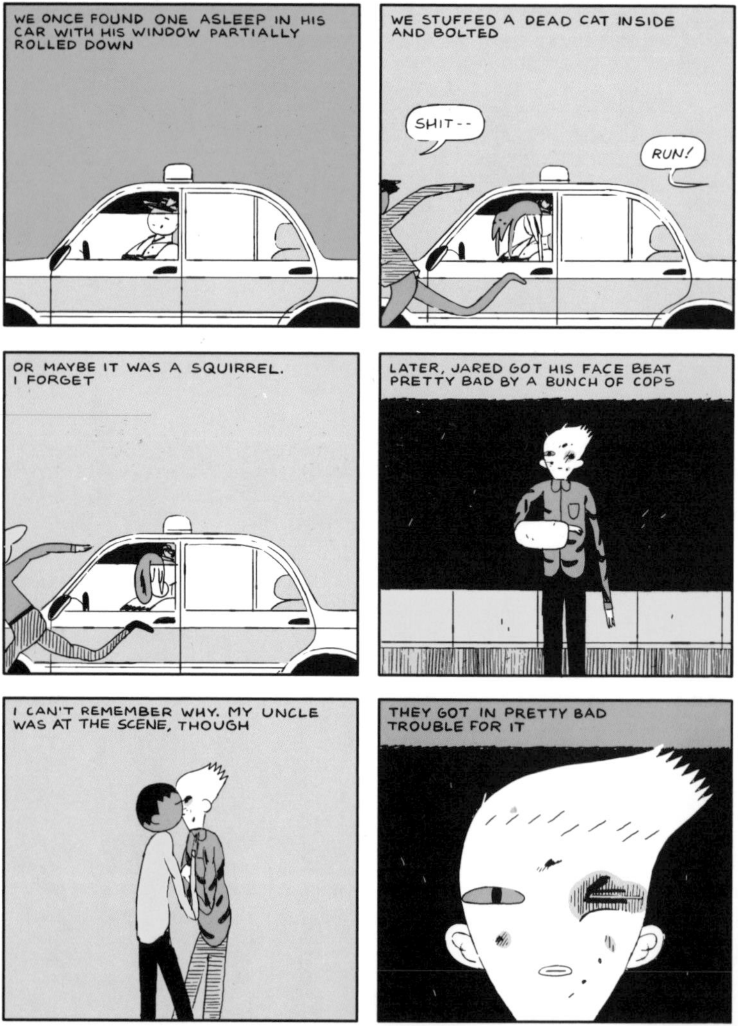
WE ONCE FOUND ONE ASLEEP IN HIS CAR WITH HIS WINDOW PARTIALLY ROLLED DOWN
WE STUFFED A DEAD CAT INSIDE AND BOLTED
SHIT--
RUN!
OR MAYBE IT WAS A SQUIRREL. I FORGET
LATER, JARED GOT HIS FACE BEAT PRETTY BAD BY A BUNCH OF COPS
I CAN'T REMEMBER WHY. MY UNCLE WAS AT THE SCENE, THOUGH
THEY GOT IN PRETTY BAD TROUBLE FOR IT

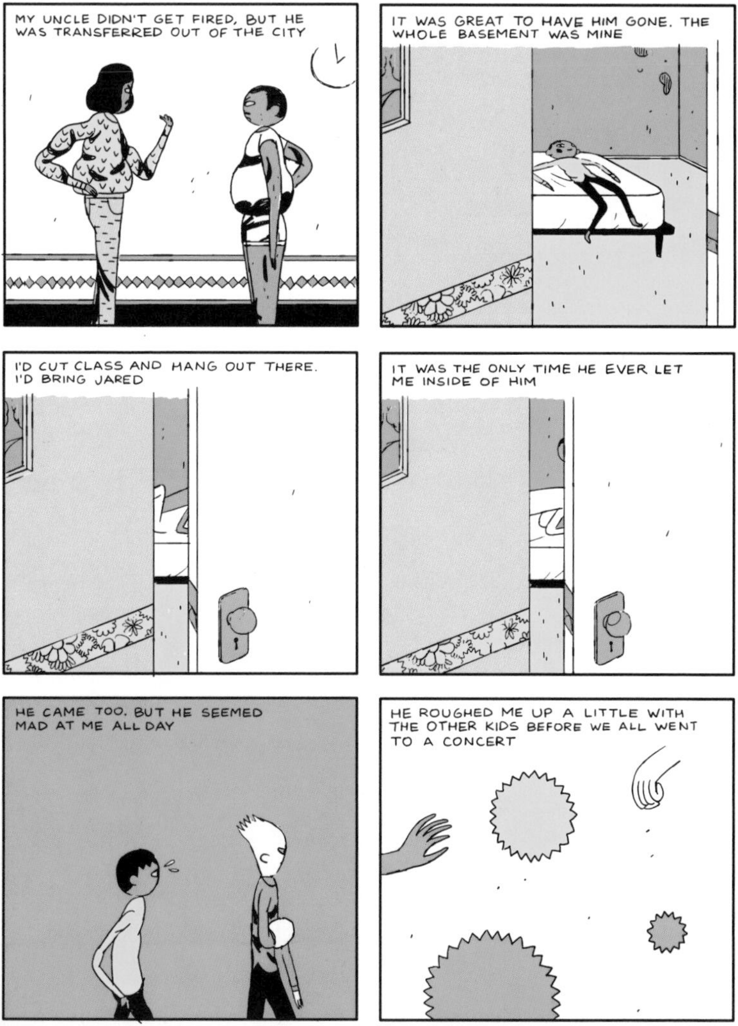
MY UNCLE DIDN'T GET FIRED, BUT HE WAS TRANSFERRED OUT OF THE CITY
IT WAS GREAT TO HAVE HIM GONE. THE WHOLE BASEMENT WAS MINE
I'D CUT CLASS AND HANG OUT THERE. I'D BRING JARED
IT WAS THE ONLY TIME HE EVER LET ME INSIDE OF HIM
HE CAME TOO. BUT HE SEEMED MAD AT ME ALL DAY
HE ROUGHED ME UP A LITTLE WITH THE OTHER KIDS BEFORE WE ALL WENT TO A CONCERT

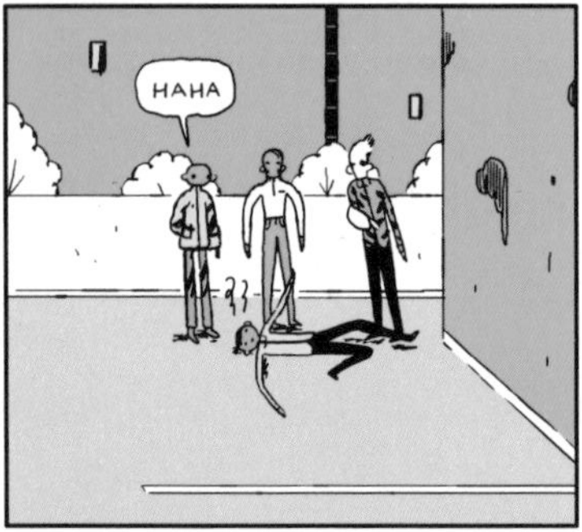
HAHA
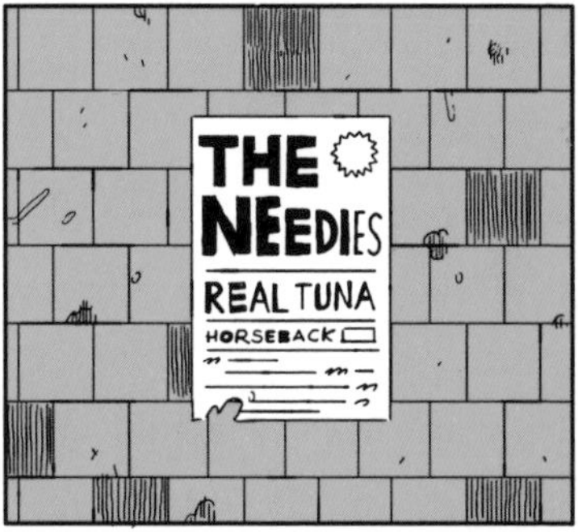
THE NEEDIES
REAL TUNA
HORSEBACK
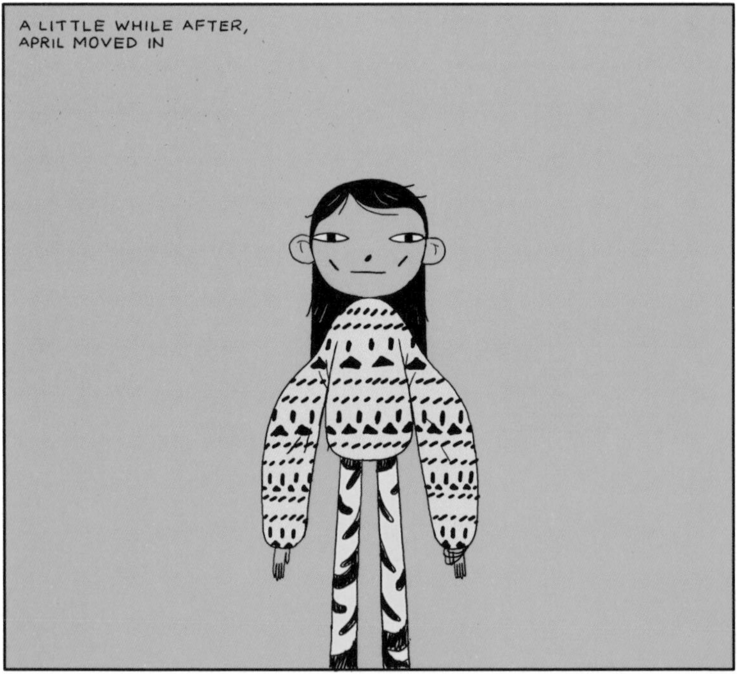
A LITTLE WHILE AFTER,
APRIL MOVED IN

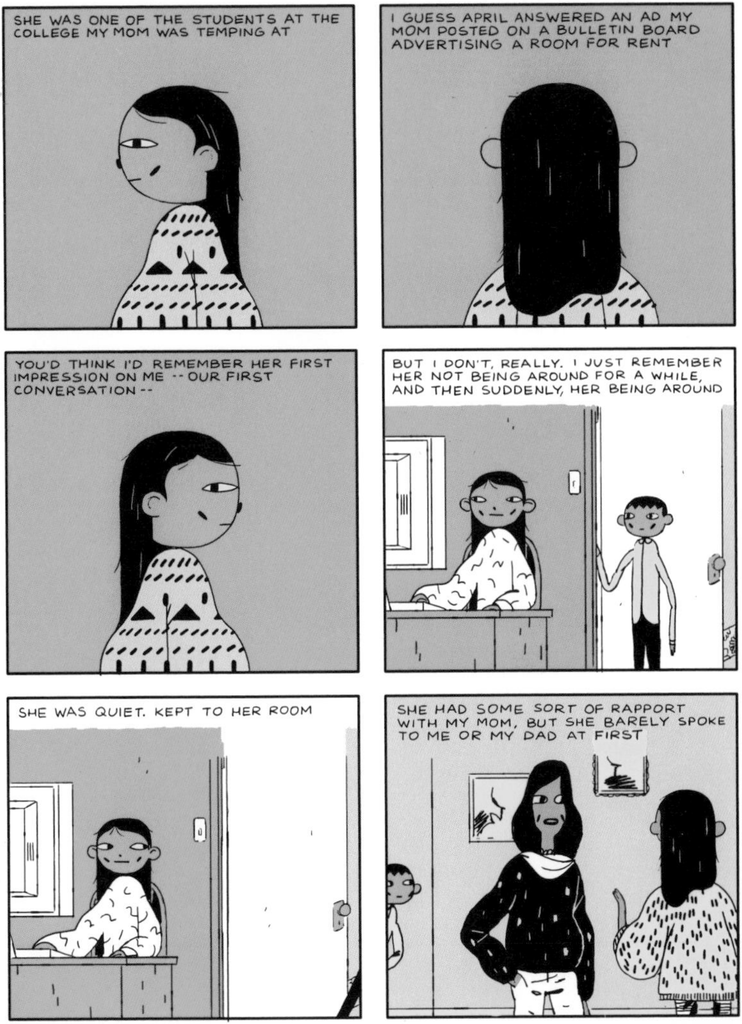
SHE WAS ONE OF THE STUDENTS AT THE COLLEGE MY MOM WAS TEMPING AT
I GUESS APRIL ANSWERED AN AD MY MOM POSTED ON A BULLETIN BOARD ADVERTISING A ROOM FOR RENT
YOU'D THINK I'D REMEMBER HER FIRST IMPRESSION ON ME -- OUR FIRST CONVERSATION --
BUT I DON'T, REALLY. I JUST REMEMBER HER NOT BEING AROUND FOR A WHILE, AND THEN SUDDENLY, HER BEING AROUND
SHE WAS QUIET. KEPT TO HER ROOM
SHE HAD SOME SORT OF RAPPORT WITH MY MOM, BUT SHE BARELY SPOKE TO ME OR MY DAD AT FIRST

SHE NEVER ATE WITH US. WE WOULD NEVER SEE HER EAT, EVEN THOUGH WE'D INVITE HER TO

SHE WAS MOSTLY ON HER COMPUTER, MAKING 3D MODELS OR SOMETHING

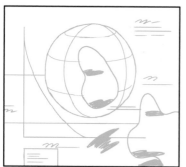

A BUNCH OF FRIENDS WERE OUT DOWNTOWN IN THE MIDDLE OF A SCHOOL DAY

DO IT

C'MON

I DON'T WANNA

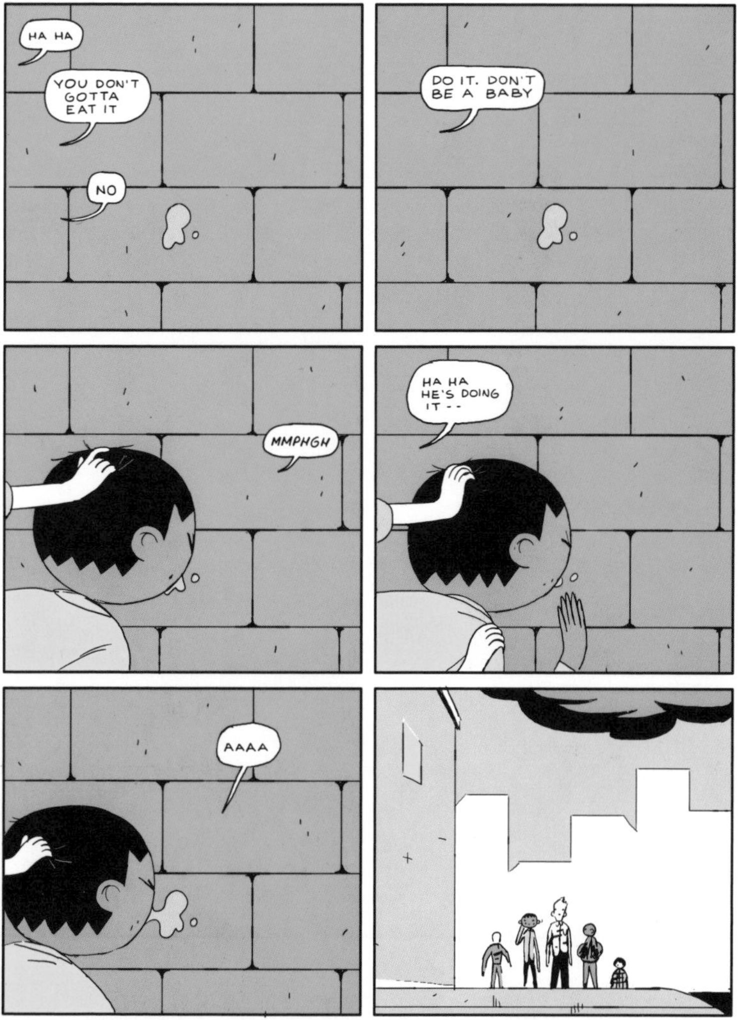
HA HA
YOU DON'T GOTTA EAT IT
NO
DO IT. DON'T BE A BABY
MMPHGH
HA HA HE'S DOING IT --
AAAA

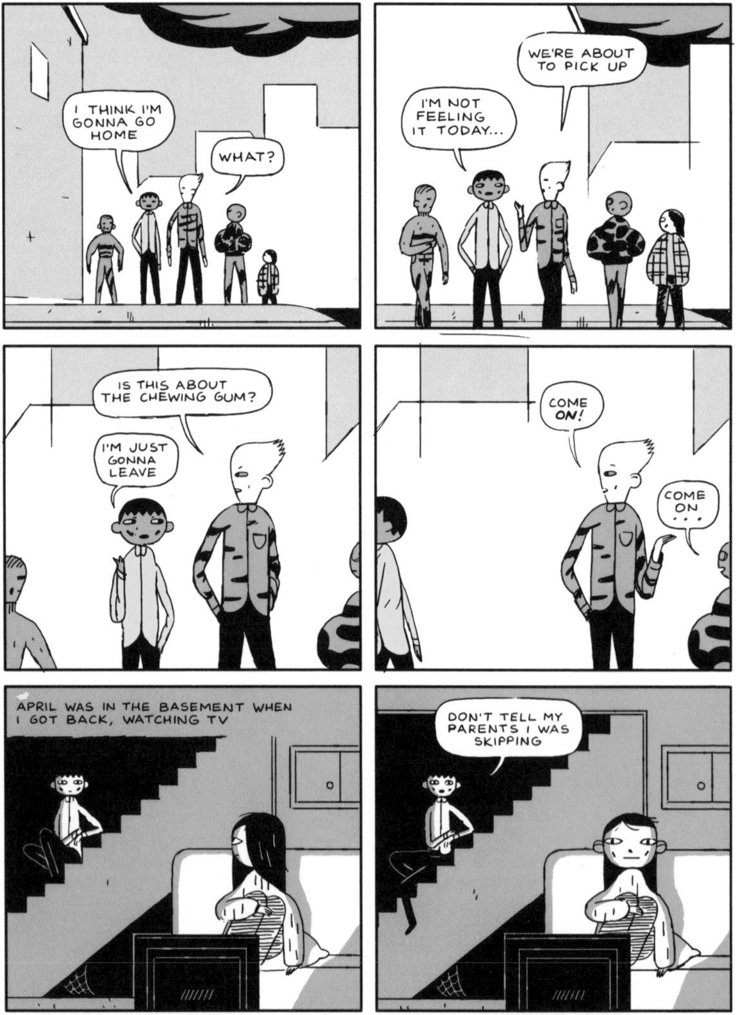
I THINK I'M GONNA GO HOME
WHAT?
I'M NOT FEELING IT TODAY...
WE'RE ABOUT TO PICK UP
IS THIS ABOUT THE CHEWING GUM?
I'M JUST GONNA LEAVE
COME ON!
COME ON . . .
APRIL WAS IN THE BASEMENT WHEN I GOT BACK, WATCHING TV
DON'T TELL MY PARENTS I WAS SKIPPING

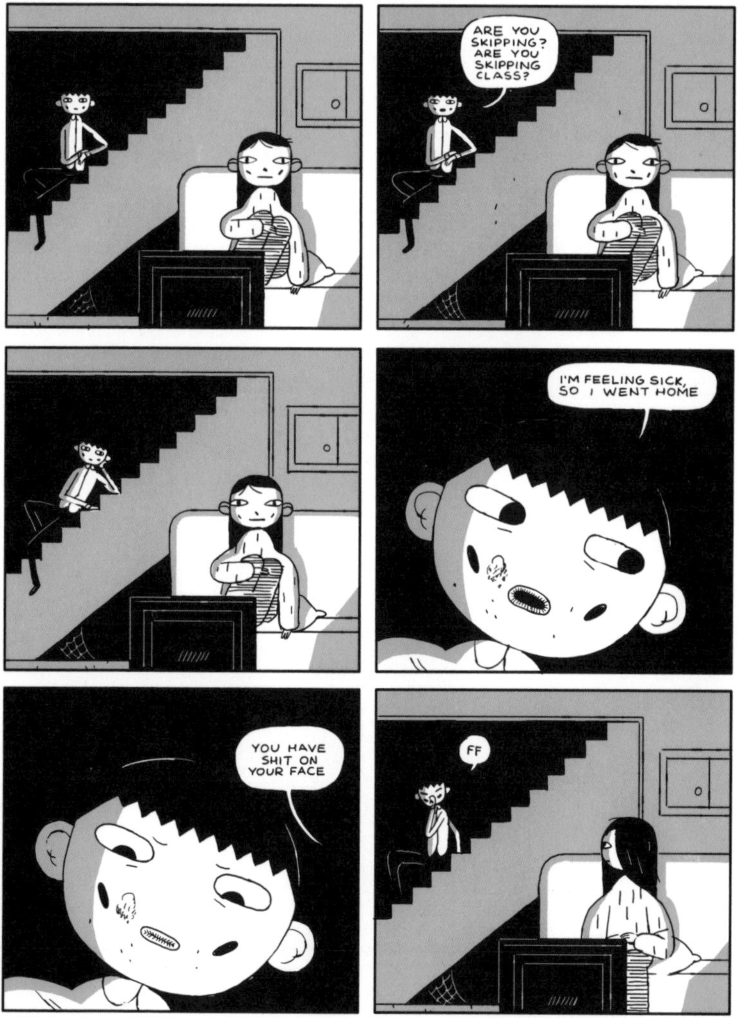
ARE YOU SKIPPING? ARE YOU SKIPPING CLASS?
I'M FEELING SICK, SO I WENT HOME
YOU HAVE SHIT ON YOUR FACE
FF

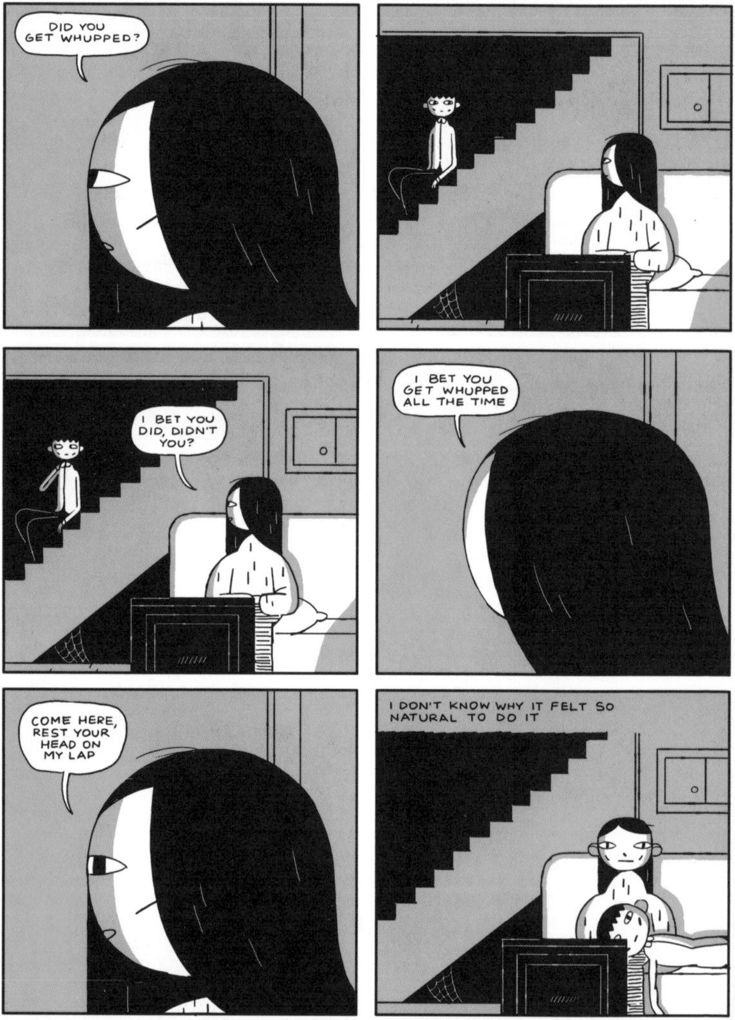
DID YOU GET WHUPPED?
I BET YOU DID, DIDN'T YOU?
I BET YOU GET WHUPPED ALL THE TIME
COME HERE, REST YOUR HEAD ON MY LAP
I DON'T KNOW WHY IT FELT SO NATURAL TO DO IT

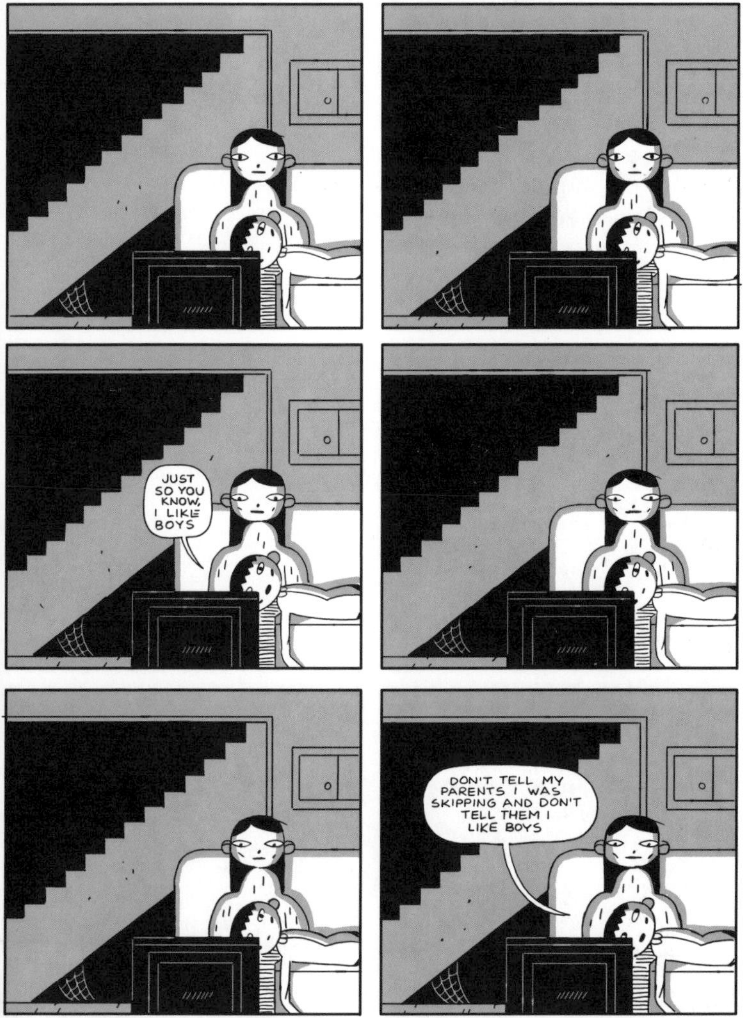
JUST SO YOU KNOW, I LIKE BOYS
DON'T TELL MY PARENTS I WAS SKIPPING AND DON'T TELL THEM I LIKE BOYS

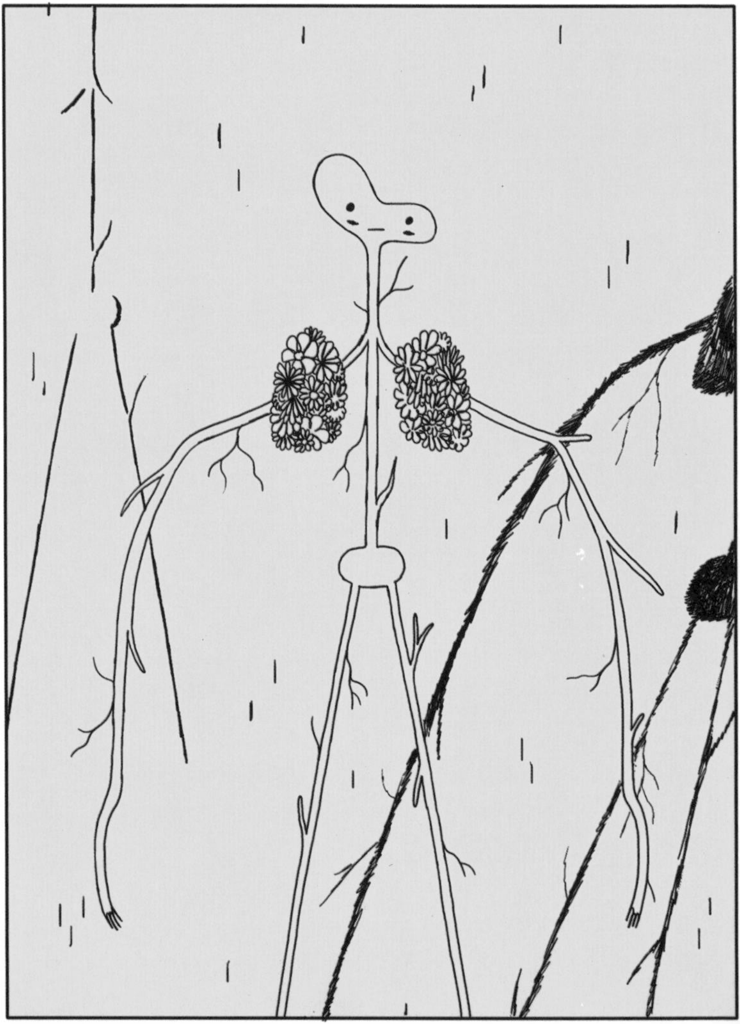

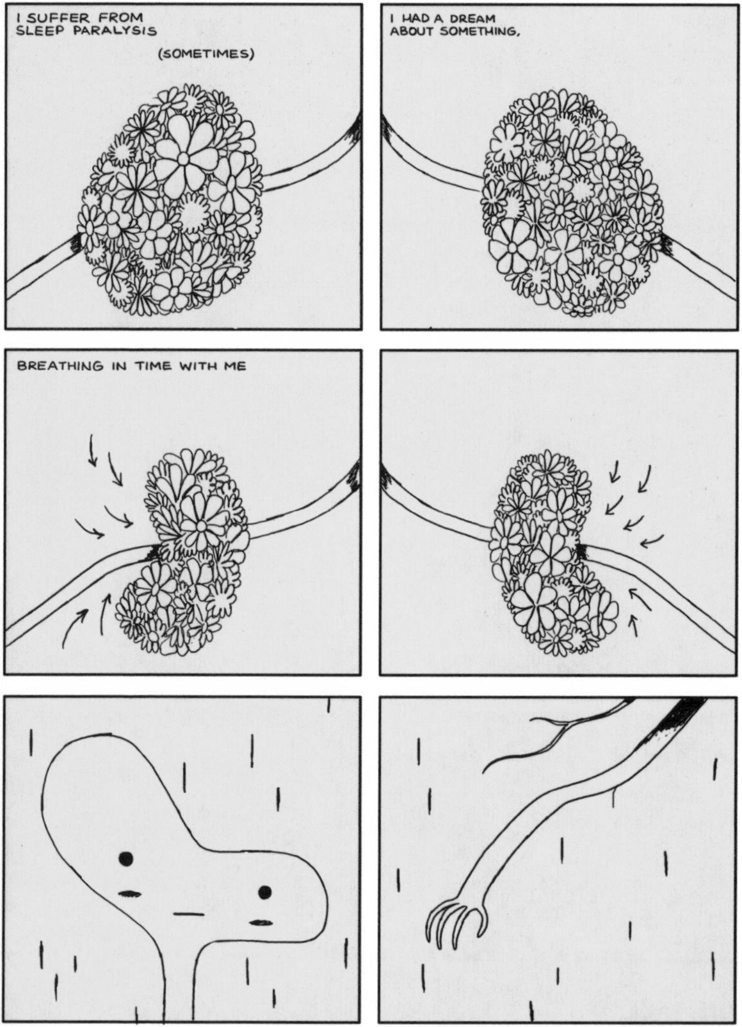
I SUFFER FROM SLEEP PARALYSIS
(SOMETIMES)
I HAD A DREAM ABOUT SOMETHING,
BREATHING IN TIME WITH ME

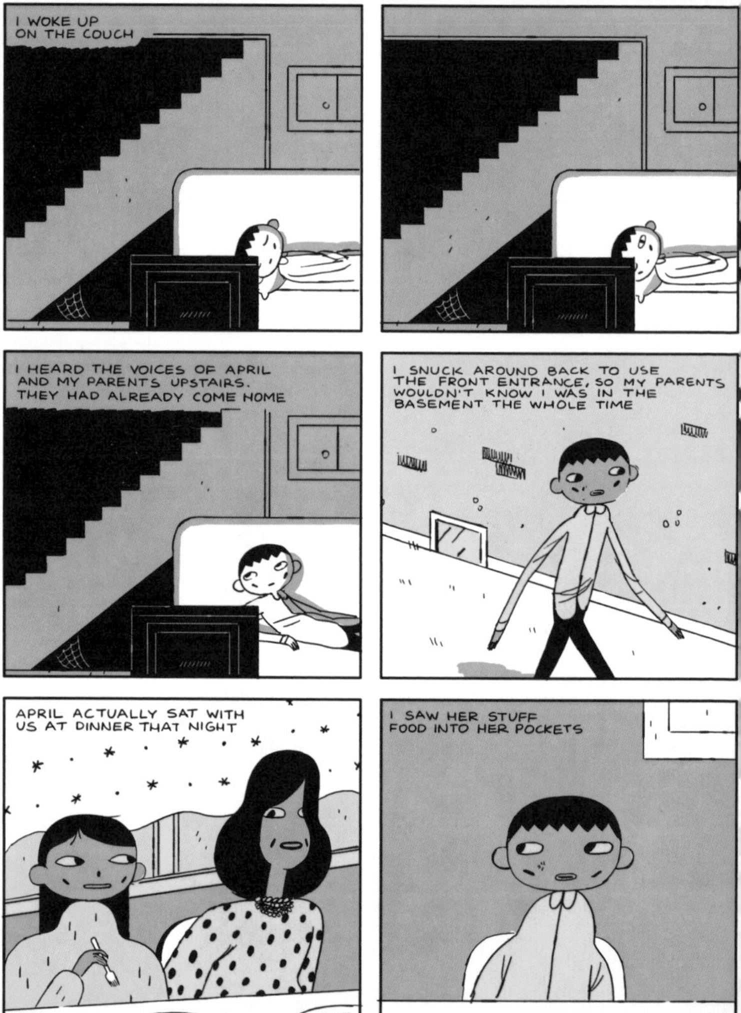
I WOKE UP
ON THE COUCH
I HEARD THE VOICES OF APRIL
AND MY PARENTS UPSTAIRS.
THEY HAD ALREADY COME HOME
I SNUCK AROUND BACK TO USE
THE FRONT ENTRANCE, SO MY PARENTS
WOULDN'T KNOW I WAS IN THE
BASEMENT THE WHOLE TIME
APRIL ACTUALLY SAT WITH
US AT DINNER THAT NIGHT
I SAW HER STUFF
FOOD INTO HER POCKETS

MORE THINGS I REMEMBER ABOUT JARED: WEIRD CUTS ON HIS LEG

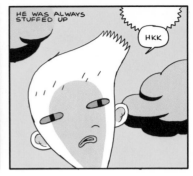
HE WAS ALWAYS STUFFED UP

HKK

HOW HE'D MAKE AN ANGRY FACE IN HIS SLEEP

BOTCHED STICK 'N' POKE

GREASY HAIR

I COULDN'T GET THE GREASE OUT OF MY PARENTS' THROW PILLOWS ONE OF THE TIMES HE CAME OVER

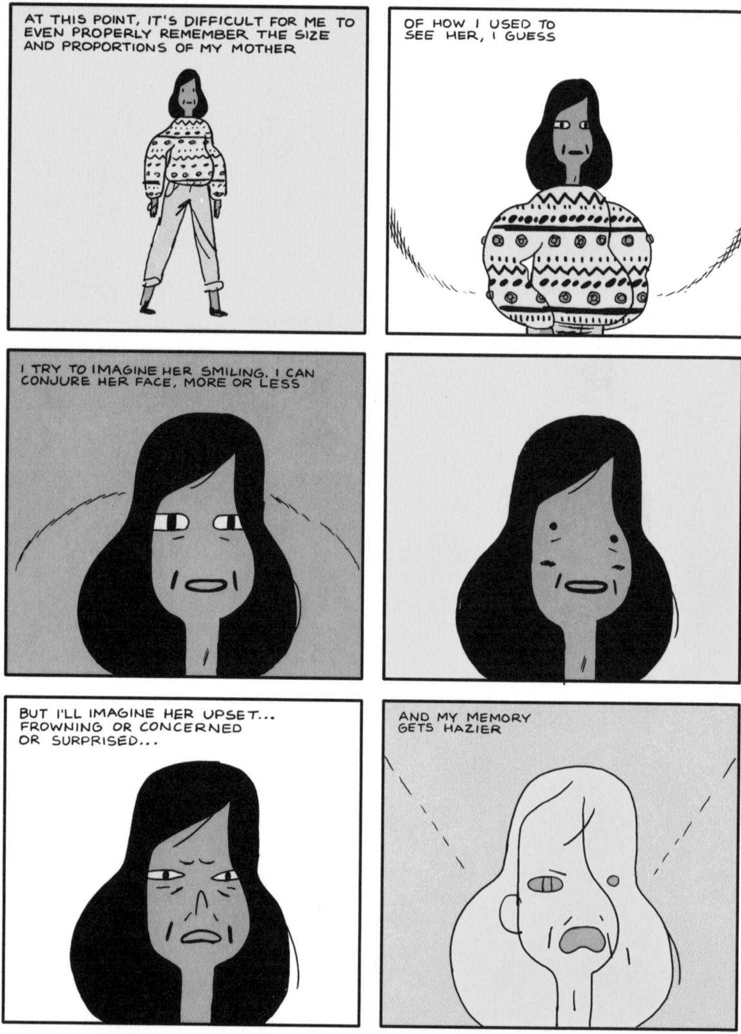
AT THIS POINT, IT'S DIFFICULT FOR ME TO EVEN PROPERLY REMEMBER THE SIZE AND PROPORTIONS OF MY MOTHER
OF HOW I USED TO SEE HER, I GUESS
I TRY TO IMAGINE HER SMILING. I CAN CONJURE HER FACE, MORE OR LESS
BUT I'LL IMAGINE HER UPSET... FROWNING OR CONCERNED OR SURPRISED...
AND MY MEMORY GETS HAZIER

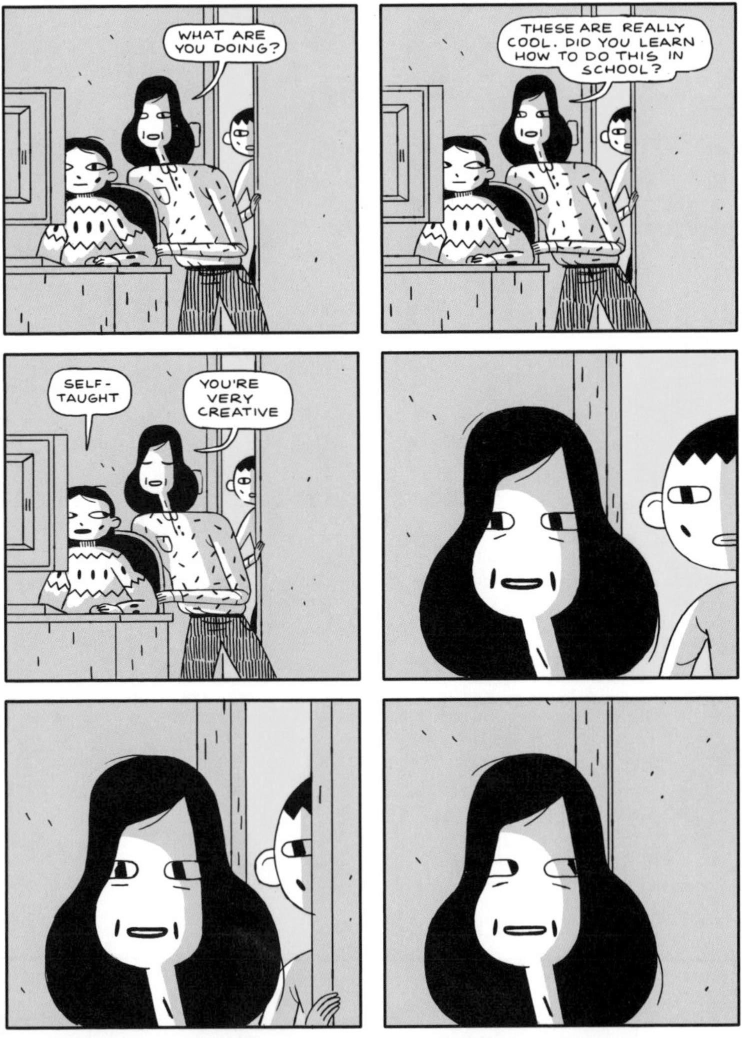
WHAT ARE YOU DOING?
THESE ARE REALLY COOL. DID YOU LEARN HOW TO DO THIS IN SCHOOL?
SELF-TAUGHT
YOU'RE VERY CREATIVE

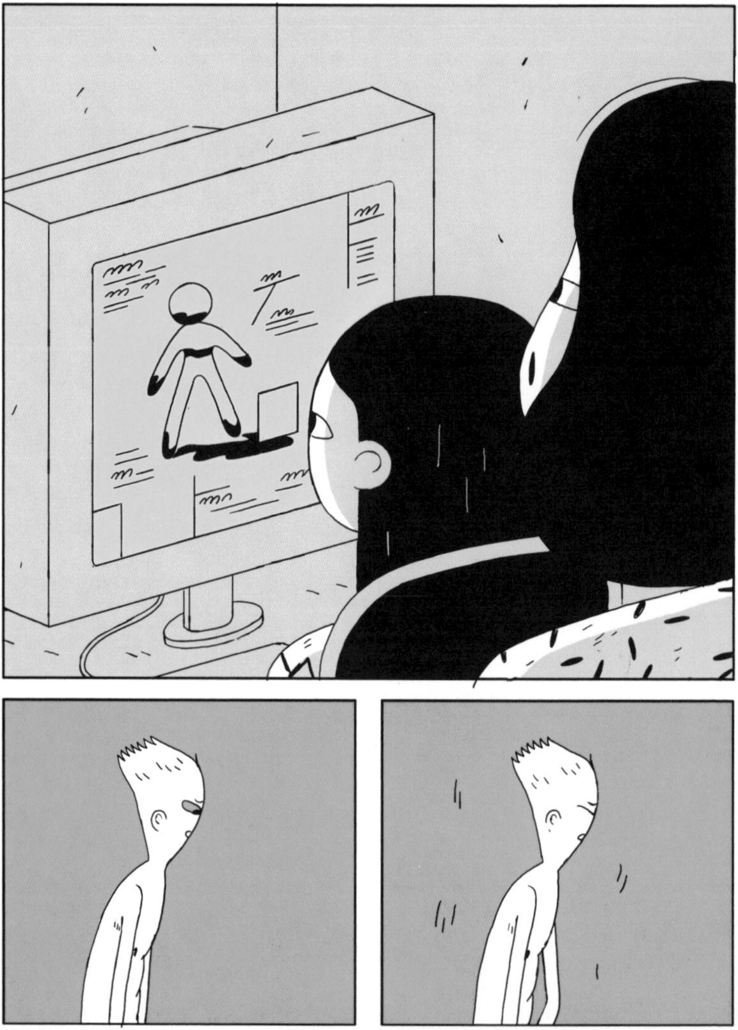

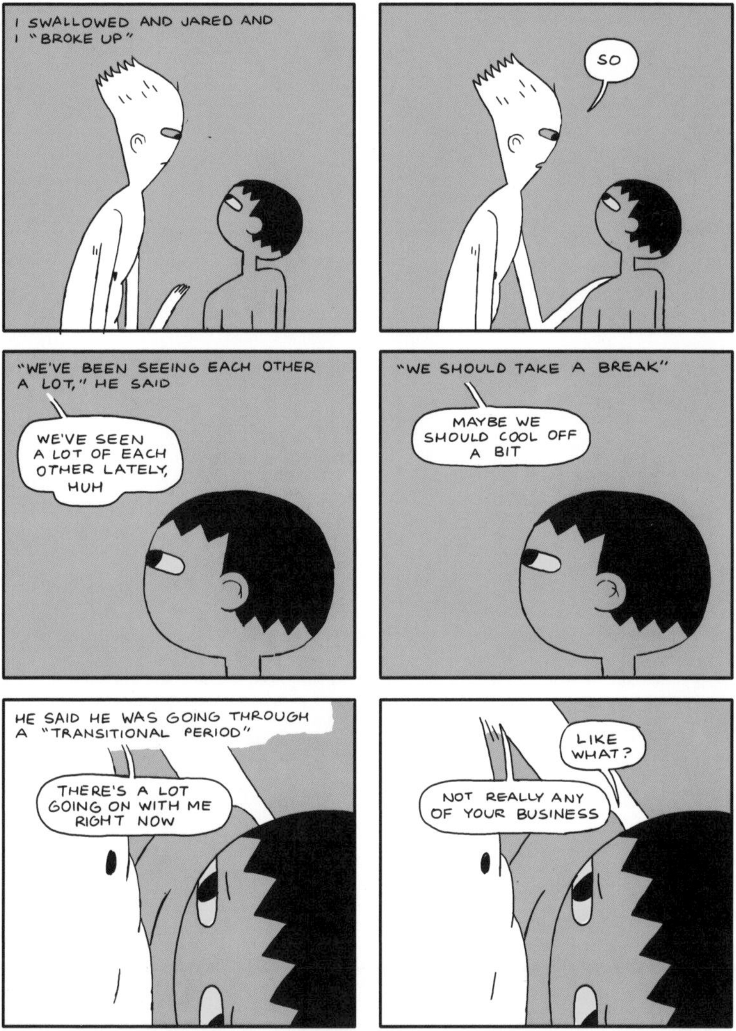
I SWALLOWED AND JARED AND I "BROKE UP"
SO
"WE'VE BEEN SEEING EACH OTHER A LOT," HE SAID
WE'VE SEEN A LOT OF EACH OTHER LATELY, HUH
"WE SHOULD TAKE A BREAK"
MAYBE WE SHOULD COOL OFF A BIT
HE SAID HE WAS GOING THROUGH A "TRANSITIONAL PERIOD"
THERE'S A LOT GOING ON WITH ME RIGHT NOW
LIKE WHAT?
NOT REALLY ANY OF YOUR BUSINESS

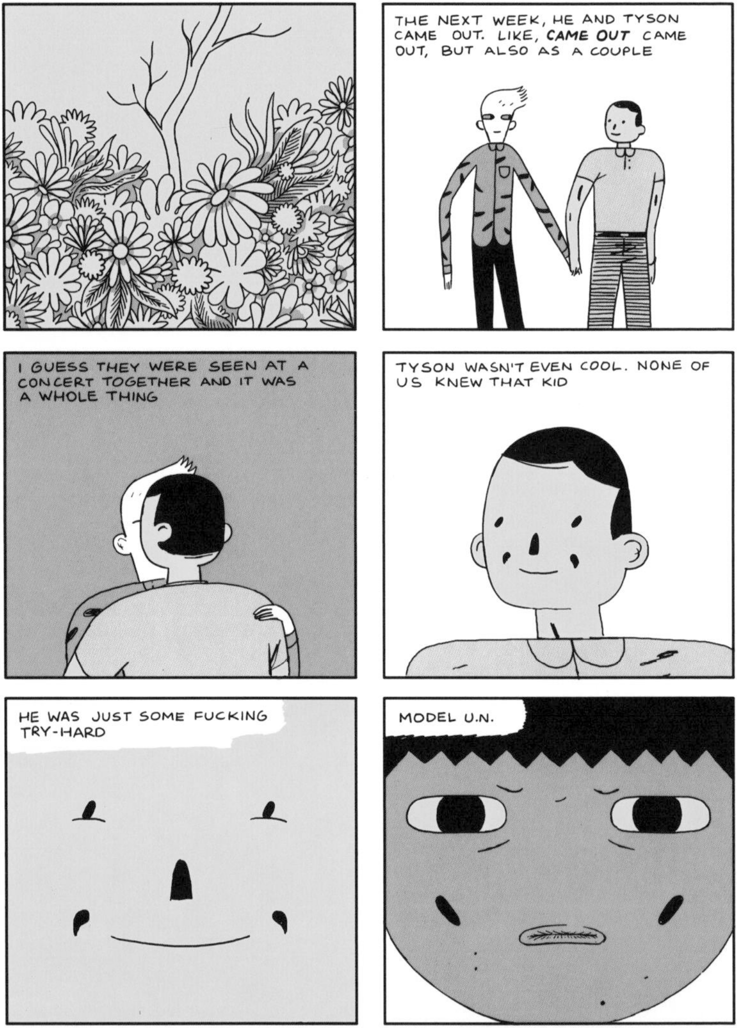
THE NEXT WEEK, HE AND TYSON CAME OUT. LIKE, **CAME OUT** CAME OUT, BUT ALSO AS A COUPLE
I GUESS THEY WERE SEEN AT A CONCERT TOGETHER AND IT WAS A WHOLE THING
TYSON WASN'T EVEN COOL. NONE OF US KNEW THAT KID
HE WAS JUST SOME FUCKING TRY-HARD
MODEL U.N.

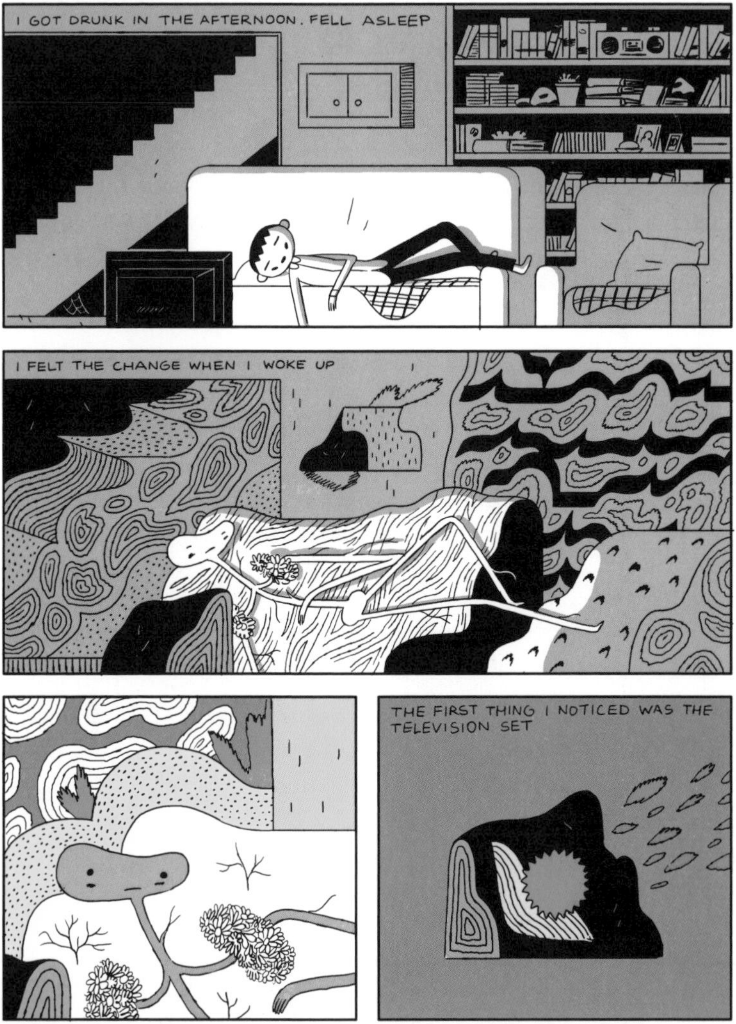
I GOT DRUNK IN THE AFTERNOON. FELL ASLEEP
I FELT THE CHANGE WHEN I WOKE UP
THE FIRST THING I NOTICED WAS THE TELEVISION SET

IT LOOKED DIFFERENT, BUT THE SAME. IT WAS IDENTICAL, BUT NOT AT ALL LIKE IT WAS BEFORE

IT STILL HAD THE SAME BUTTONS

I RECOGNIZED THE CHANNEL, THE SHOW PLAYING

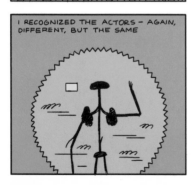

I RECOGNIZED THE ACTORS — AGAIN, DIFFERENT, BUT THE SAME

EVEN THE WAY THE LIGHT SHONE AGAINST OBJECTS IN THE ROOM HAD CHANGED

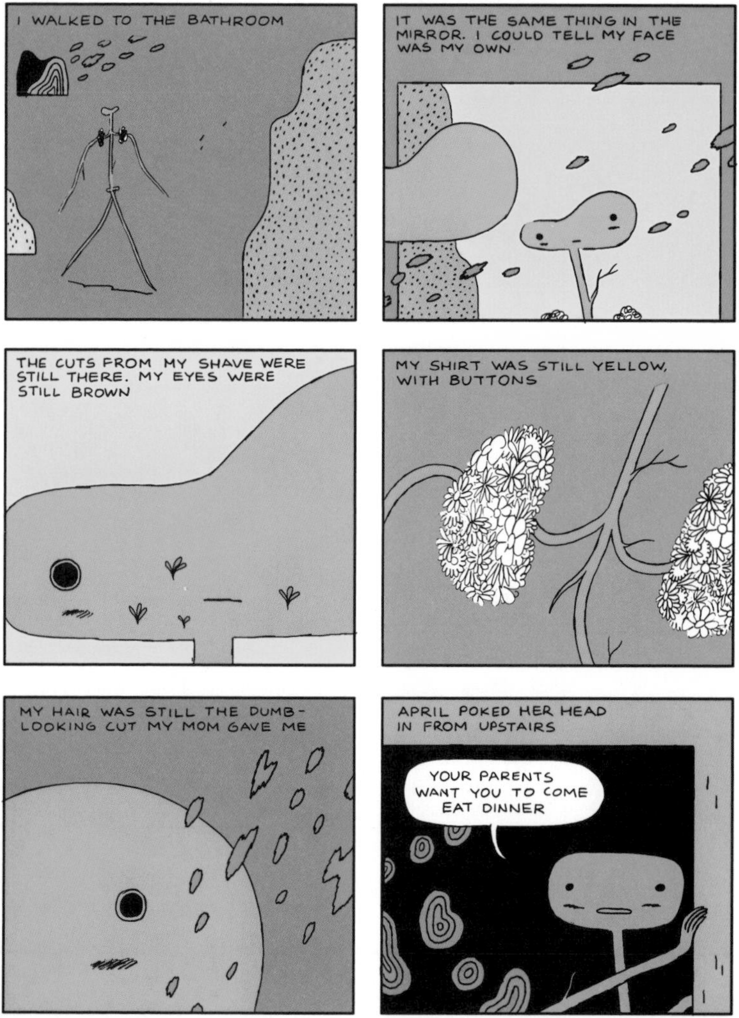
I WALKED TO THE BATHROOM
IT WAS THE SAME THING IN THE MIRROR. I COULD TELL MY FACE WAS MY OWN
THE CUTS FROM MY SHAVE WERE STILL THERE. MY EYES WERE STILL BROWN
MY SHIRT WAS STILL YELLOW, WITH BUTTONS
MY HAIR WAS STILL THE DUMB-LOOKING CUT MY MOM GAVE ME
APRIL POKED HER HEAD IN FROM UPSTAIRS
YOUR PARENTS WANT YOU TO COME EAT DINNER

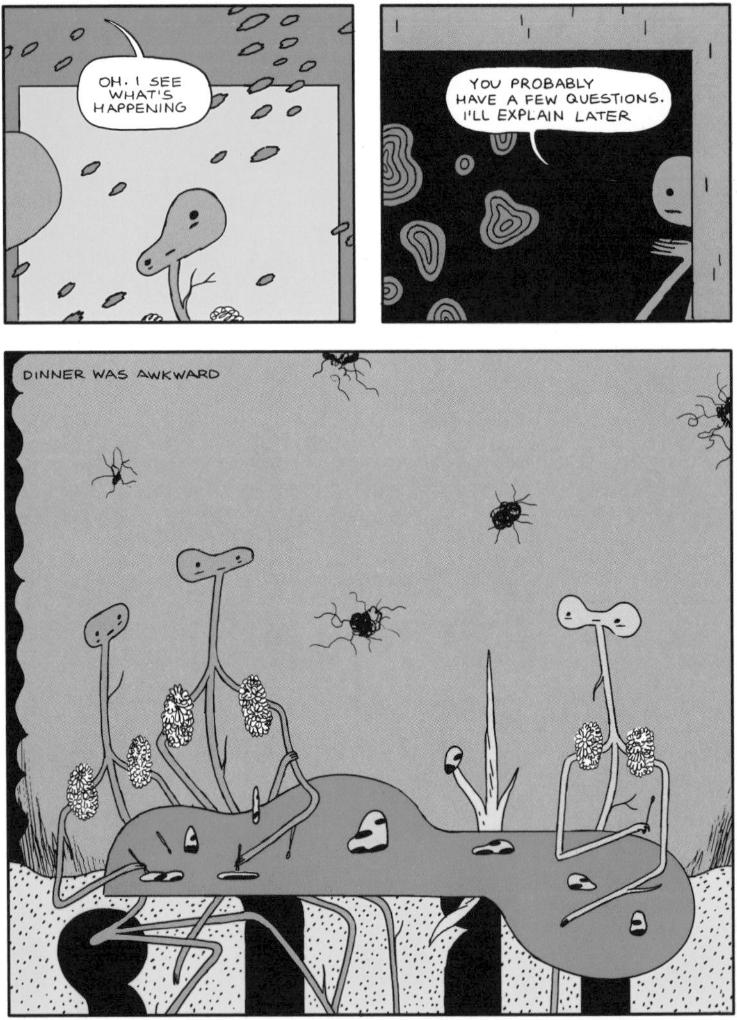
OH. I SEE WHAT'S HAPPENING
YOU PROBABLY HAVE A FEW QUESTIONS. I'LL EXPLAIN LATER
DINNER WAS AWKWARD

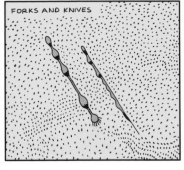

FORKS AND KNIVES

PLATES OF FOOD

THE WAY FOOD TASTED

THE WAY WATER TASTED

MOM

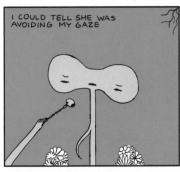

I COULD TELL SHE WAS AVOIDING MY GAZE

APRIL. ALL THE STUDENTS IN MY CLASSES ARE VERY EXCITED ABOUT THE ATHLETIC CENTRE'S POOL BEING REOPENED. ARE YOU?
MAYBE YOU TWO SHOULD GO TO THE POOL
SHE WOULDN'T MAKE EYE CONTACT
THE LAMB IS ESPECIALLY GOOD TONIGHT
SHE SEEMED SO TENSE
THANK YOU
DAD
VERY, VERY GOOD

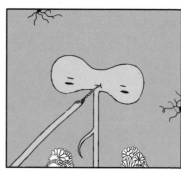

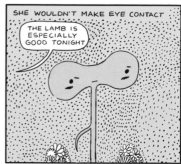

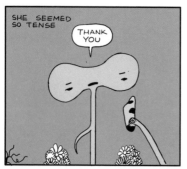

MY DAD HAD CHANGED, TOO... BUT IN A DIFFERENT WAY I COULDN'T QUITE PLACE MY FINGER ON

SPEAKING OF SCHOOL, HOW ARE YOU LIKING THE SEMESTER?

WE'RE STILL HOPING THAT A CERTAIN *SOMEONE* BEGINS TO START THINKING ABOUT COLLEGE APPLICATIONS

DAD

HE LOOKED MORE OPAQUE TO ME, SOMEHOW

NOT MANY KNOW THAT BARTLEBY HAS AN EXCELLENT JOURNALISM PROGRAM. MY EDITOR WENT TO BARTLEBY

DO YOU HAVE PROFESSOR CAUL THIS YEAR? I ONCE INTERVIEWED HIM FOR A PIECE ON ROBOTICS PATENTS. HE'S LOVELY

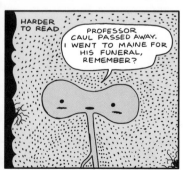

HARDER TO READ

PROFESSOR CAUL PASSED AWAY. I WENT TO MAINE FOR HIS FUNERAL, REMEMBER?

SCHOOL IS FINE

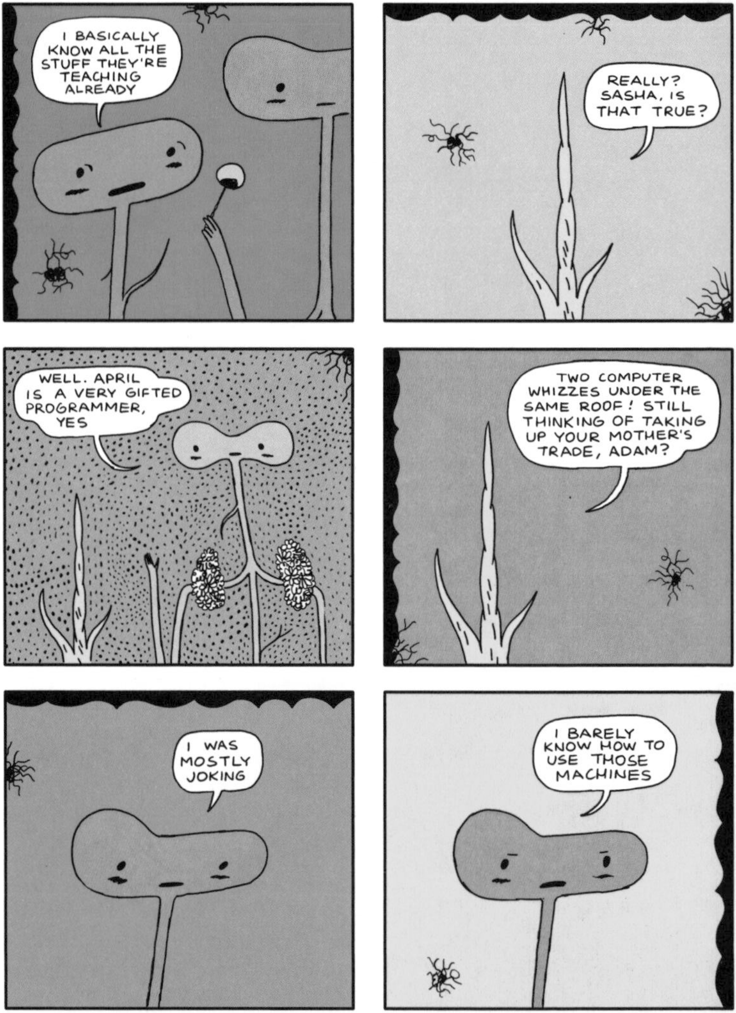
I BASICALLY KNOW ALL THE STUFF THEY'RE TEACHING ALREADY
REALLY? SASHA, IS THAT TRUE?
WELL. APRIL IS A VERY GIFTED PROGRAMMER, YES
TWO COMPUTER WHIZZES UNDER THE SAME ROOF! STILL THINKING OF TAKING UP YOUR MOTHER'S TRADE, ADAM?
I WAS MOSTLY JOKING
I BARELY KNOW HOW TO USE THOSE MACHINES

I DIDN'T GET WHY EVERYONE WAS ACTING NORMAL

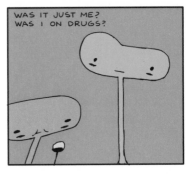

WAS IT JUST ME? WAS I ON DRUGS?

IT WASN'T EXACTLY LIKE DRUGS. NOTHING SEEMED *LESS* REAL. THE OPPOSITE, IN FACT

LIKE I HAD JUST BEEN LISTENING TO A BAND PLAYING FROM A BAR'S BATHROOM AND THE MUSIC WAS COMING OUT ALL MUFFLED... BUT SUDDENLY, I WAS ON THE CONCERT FLOOR, AND ALL THE MELODIES WERE CRISP AND CLEAR

CHEWING NOISES

THERE WAS AN ENERGY COMING OFF OF EVERYTHING. THE CUPBOARD AND ITS CONTENTS, STILL

THE WINDOW'S CURTAINS, FLAPPING

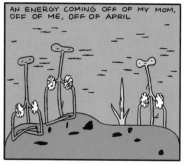

AN ENERGY COMING OFF OF MY MOM, OFF OF ME, OFF OF APRIL

FUZZY LITTLE BEAMS THAT WORMED ONTO OUR BODIES

BURROWING INTO OUR FLOWER BEDS

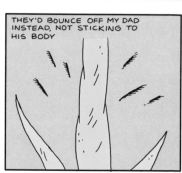

THEY'D BOUNCE OFF MY DAD INSTEAD, NOT STICKING TO HIS BODY

FORMING A HALO AROUND HIM

GIVING HIM A SORT OF DOPEY, DUMBSTRUCK LOOK

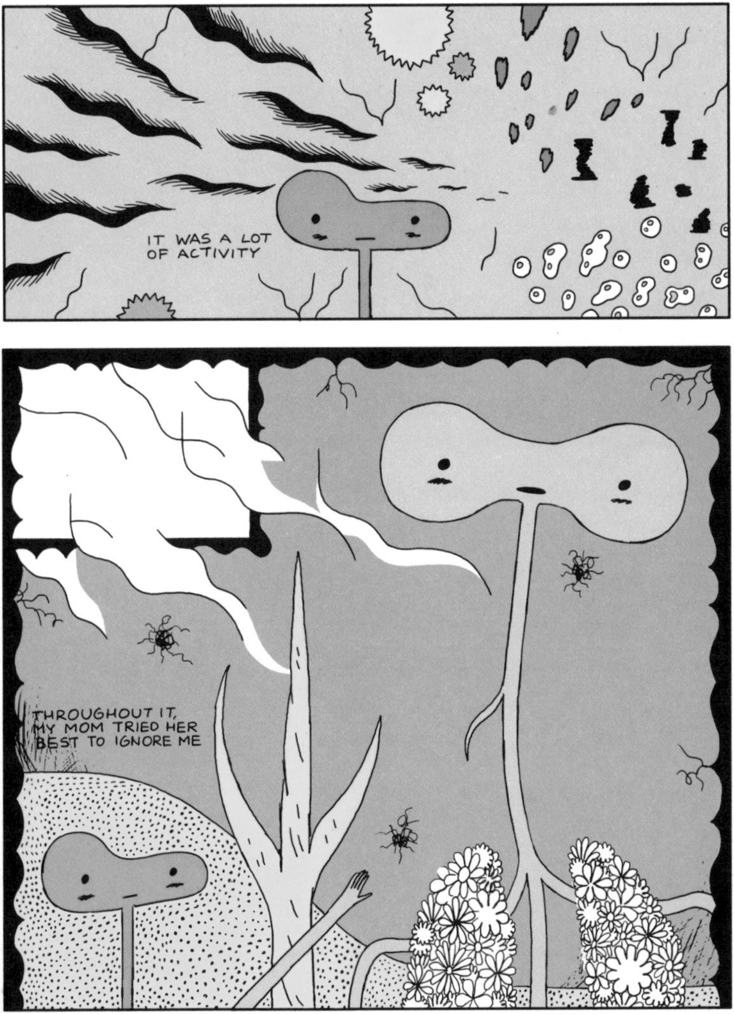
IT WAS A LOT OF ACTIVITY
THROUGHOUT IT, MY MOM TRIED HER BEST TO IGNORE ME

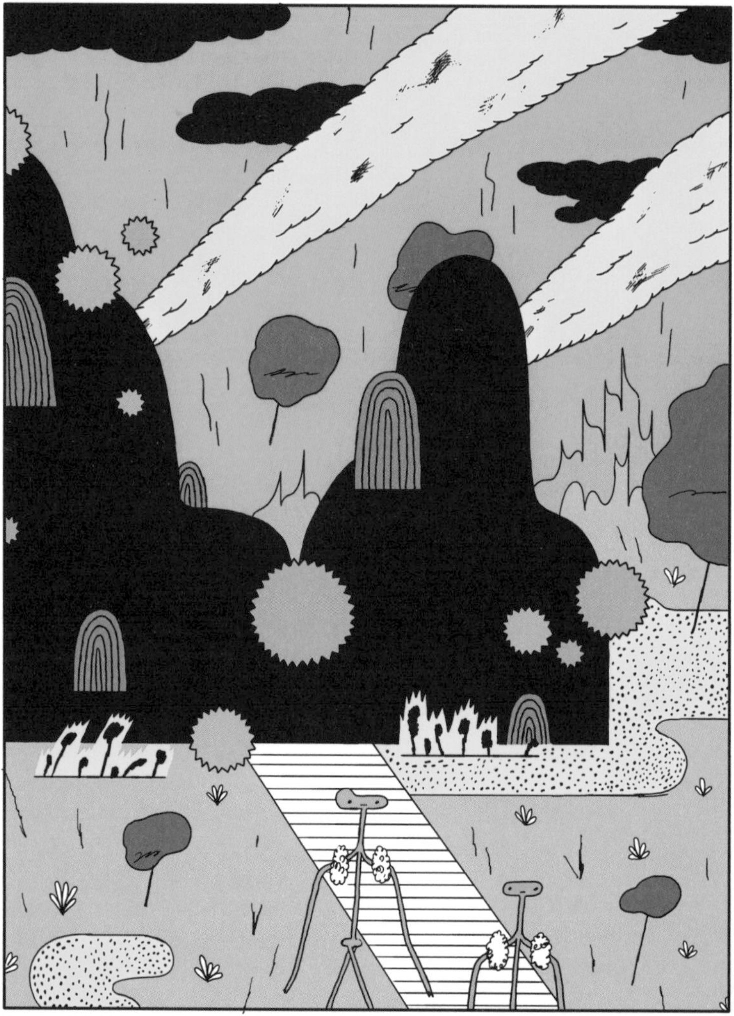

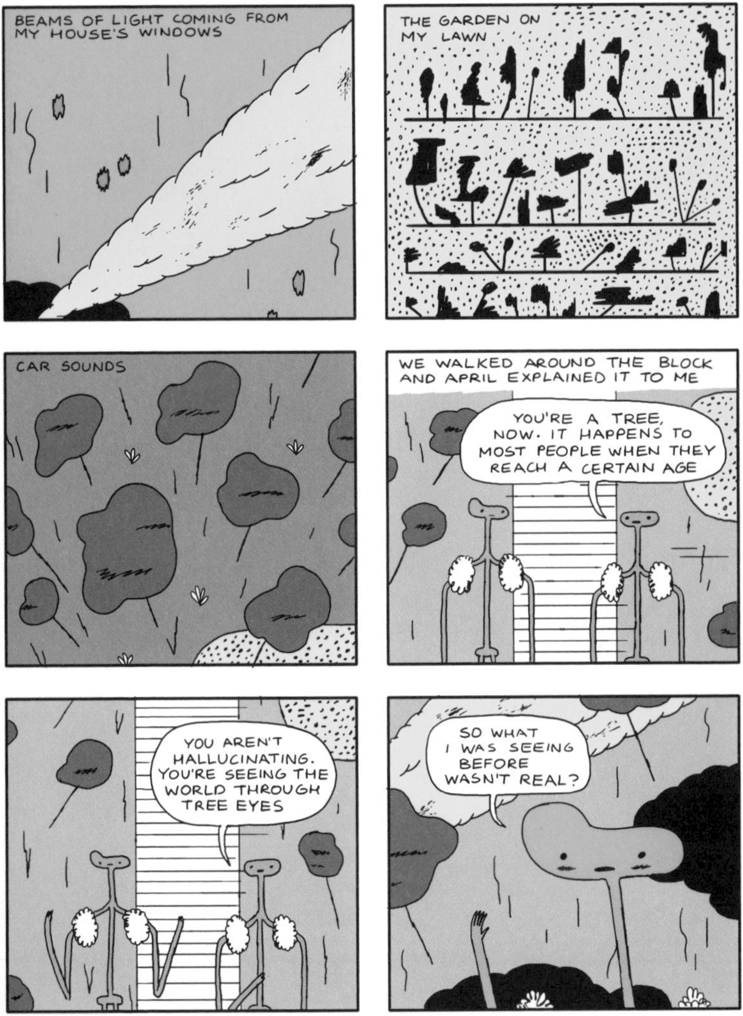
BEAMS OF LIGHT COMING FROM MY HOUSE'S WINDOWS
THE GARDEN ON MY LAWN
CAR SOUNDS
WE WALKED AROUND THE BLOCK AND APRIL EXPLAINED IT TO ME
YOU'RE A TREE, NOW. IT HAPPENS TO MOST PEOPLE WHEN THEY REACH A CERTAIN AGE
YOU AREN'T HALLUCINATING. YOU'RE SEEING THE WORLD THROUGH TREE EYES
SO WHAT I WAS SEEING BEFORE WASN'T REAL?

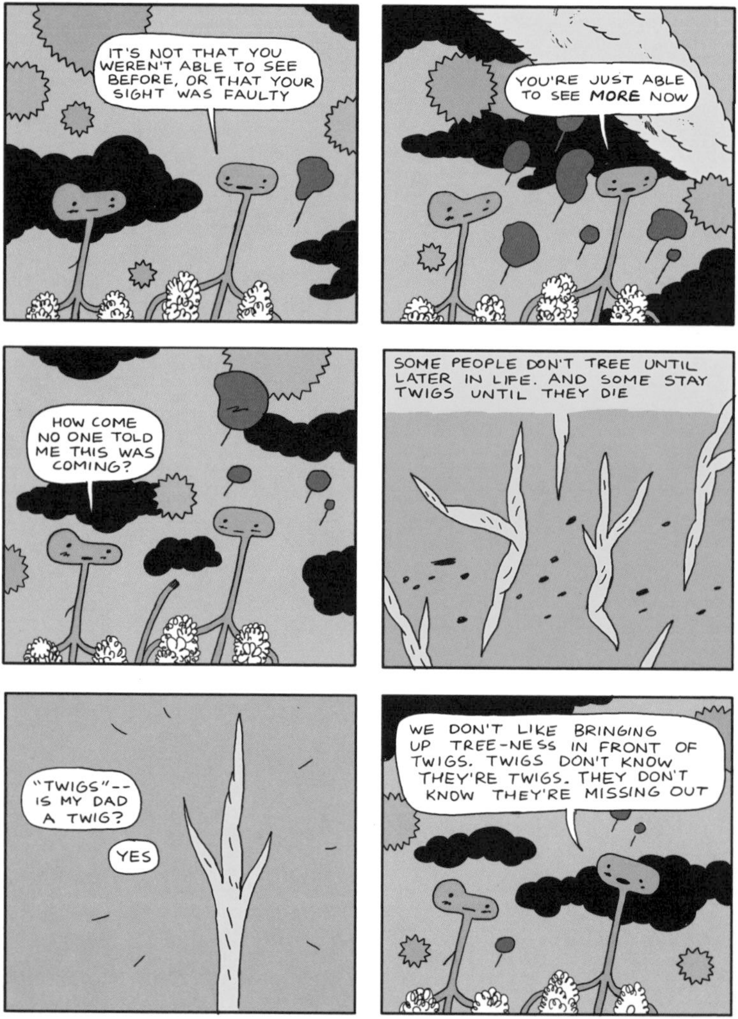
IT'S NOT THAT YOU WEREN'T ABLE TO SEE BEFORE, OR THAT YOUR SIGHT WAS FAULTY
YOU'RE JUST ABLE TO SEE MORE NOW
HOW COME NO ONE TOLD ME THIS WAS COMING?
SOME PEOPLE DON'T TREE UNTIL LATER IN LIFE. AND SOME STAY TWIGS UNTIL THEY DIE
"TWIGS"-- IS MY DAD A TWIG?
YES
WE DON'T LIKE BRINGING UP TREE-NESS IN FRONT OF TWIGS. TWIGS DON'T KNOW THEY'RE TWIGS. THEY DON'T KNOW THEY'RE MISSING OUT

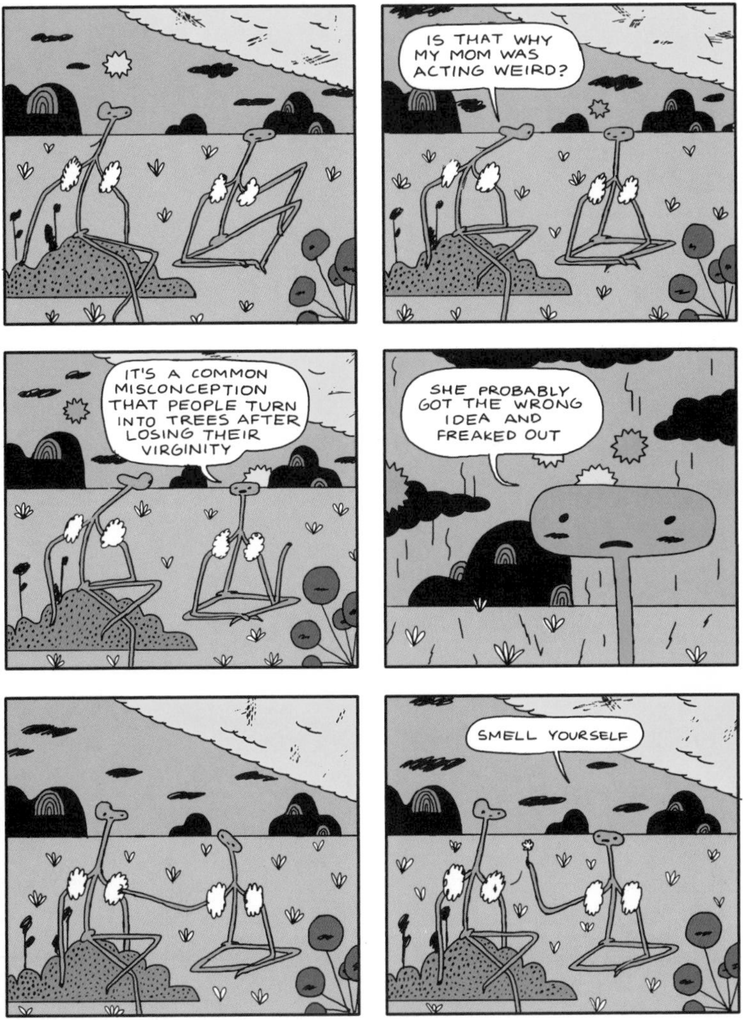
IS THAT WHY MY MOM WAS ACTING WEIRD?
IT'S A COMMON MISCONCEPTION THAT PEOPLE TURN INTO TREES AFTER LOSING THEIR VIRGINITY
SHE PROBABLY GOT THE WRONG IDEA AND FREAKED OUT
SMELL YOURSELF

IT SMELLED
LIKE THIS

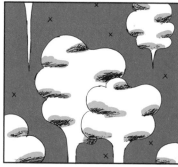

WE TALKED A LITTLE LONGER

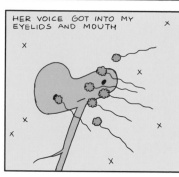

HER VOICE GOT INTO MY
EYELIDS AND MOUTH

UNDER MY BLANKET THAT NIGHT

I GOT A SONG
STUCK IN MY HEAD

THE BASS FIRST. THEN THE DRUMS

THEN THE WEIRD STOP-START GUITAR RIFF CAME TO ME

THEN ITS DEVIL HORNS

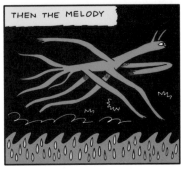

THEN THE MELODY

CHORUS

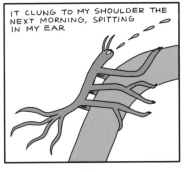

IT CLUNG TO MY SHOULDER THE NEXT MORNING, SPITTING IN MY EAR

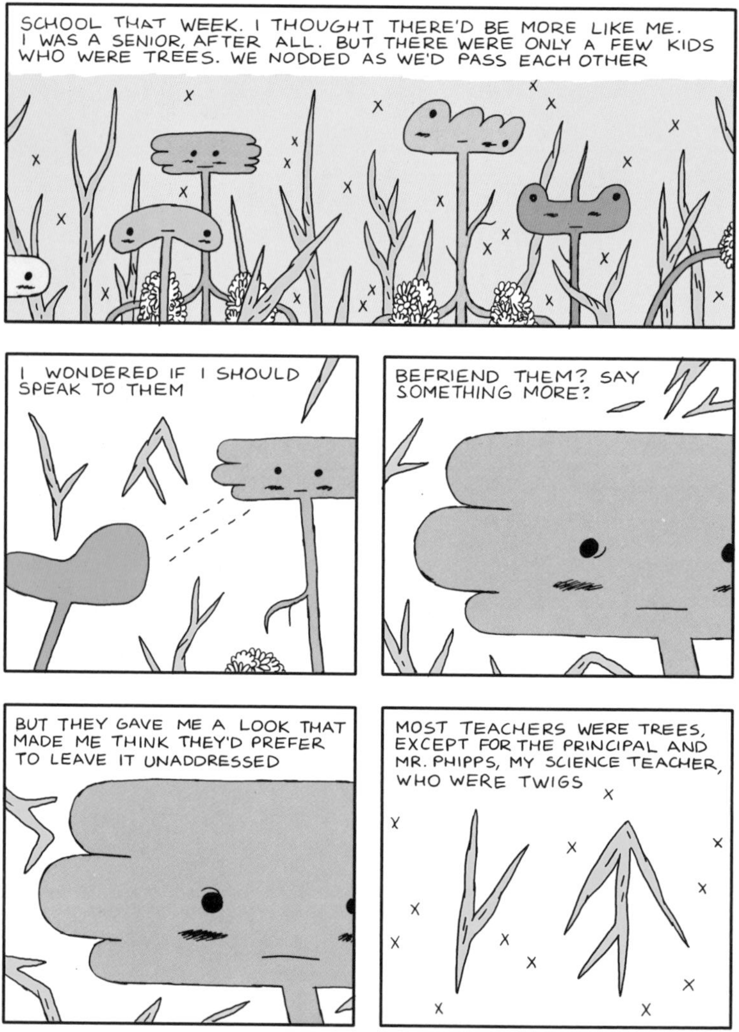
SCHOOL THAT WEEK. I THOUGHT THERE'D BE MORE LIKE ME. I WAS A SENIOR, AFTER ALL. BUT THERE WERE ONLY A FEW KIDS WHO WERE TREES. WE NODDED AS WE'D PASS EACH OTHER
I WONDERED IF I SHOULD SPEAK TO THEM
BEFRIEND THEM? SAY SOMETHING MORE?
BUT THEY GAVE ME A LOOK THAT MADE ME THINK THEY'D PREFER TO LEAVE IT UNADDRESSED
MOST TEACHERS WERE TREES, EXCEPT FOR THE PRINCIPAL AND MR. PHIPPS, MY SCIENCE TEACHER, WHO WERE TWIGS

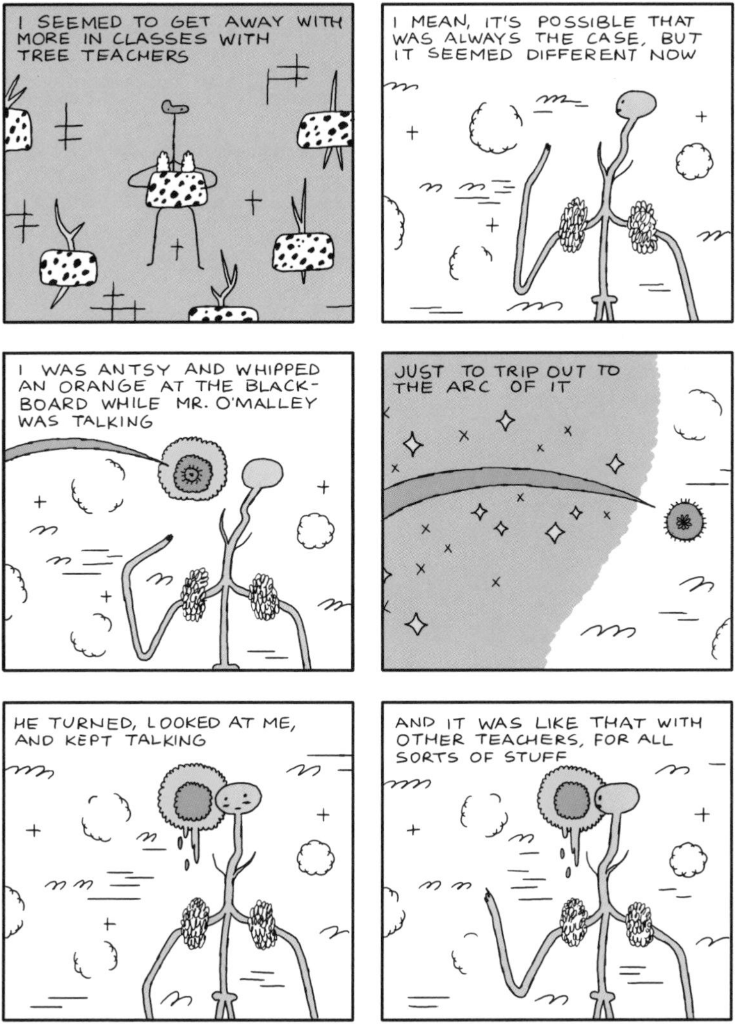
I SEEMED TO GET AWAY WITH MORE IN CLASSES WITH TREE TEACHERS
I MEAN, IT'S POSSIBLE THAT WAS ALWAYS THE CASE, BUT IT SEEMED DIFFERENT NOW
I WAS ANTSY AND WHIPPED AN ORANGE AT THE BLACK-BOARD WHILE MR. O'MALLEY WAS TALKING
JUST TO TRIP OUT TO THE ARC OF IT
HE TURNED, LOOKED AT ME, AND KEPT TALKING
AND IT WAS LIKE THAT WITH OTHER TEACHERS, FOR ALL SORTS OF STUFF

IT'S NOT LIKE I FELT ANY MORE AFFECTION FROM THEM

BUT IT WAS CLEAR I WAS NO LONGER A "PROBLEM CHILD"

THEY STOPPED WORRYING ABOUT MY BRUISES AND MY ATTENTION SPAN

STOPPED GETTING UPSET WITH MY OUTBURSTS OR ABSENCES

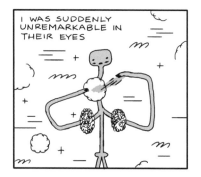

I WAS SUDDENLY UNREMARKABLE IN THEIR EYES

MEANWHILE

I WAS TRYING OUT TREE LIFE. I ATE FOOD I HATED JUST TO TASTE IT WITH NEW TASTE BUDS

I JABBED A PENCIL INTO MY LEG IN ORDER TO SEE STARS

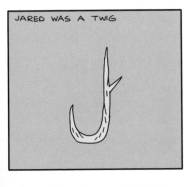

ALL MY FRIENDS WERE TWIGS, IT TURNS OUT

I FELT GROSS TALKING TO THEM. THEIR SHAPES GROSSED ME OUT

JARED WAS A TWIG

ALTHOUGH HE WASN'T FRIENDS WITH ALL MY FRIENDS ANYMORE, ON ACCOUNT OF HIM BEING A FAG

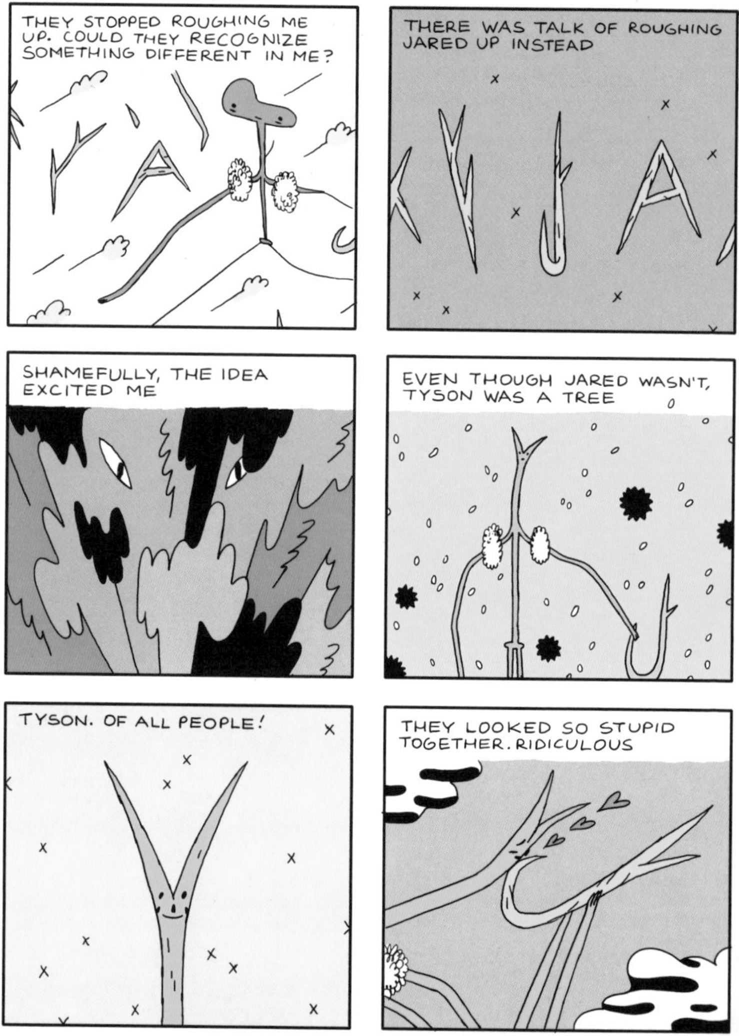
THEY STOPPED ROUGHING ME UP. COULD THEY RECOGNIZE SOMETHING DIFFERENT IN ME?
THERE WAS TALK OF ROUGHING JARED UP INSTEAD
SHAMEFULLY, THE IDEA EXCITED ME
EVEN THOUGH JARED WASN'T, TYSON WAS A TREE
TYSON. OF ALL PEOPLE!
THEY LOOKED SO STUPID TOGETHER. RIDICULOUS

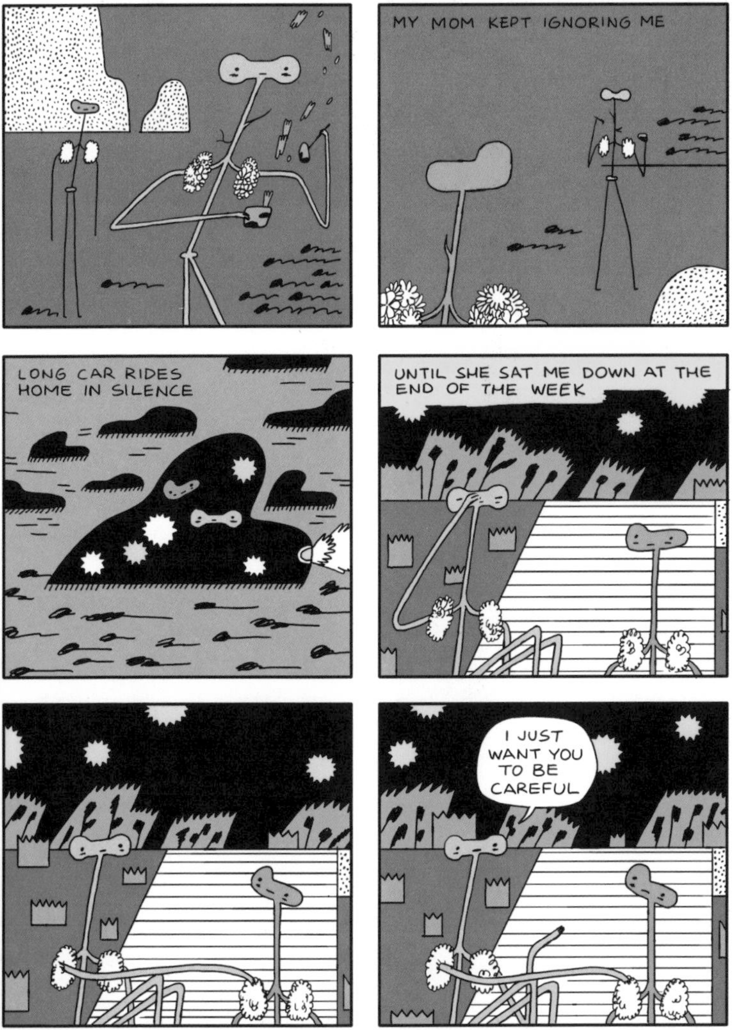
MY MOM KEPT IGNORING ME
LONG CAR RIDES HOME IN SILENCE
UNTIL SHE SAT ME DOWN AT THE END OF THE WEEK
I JUST WANT YOU TO BE CAREFUL

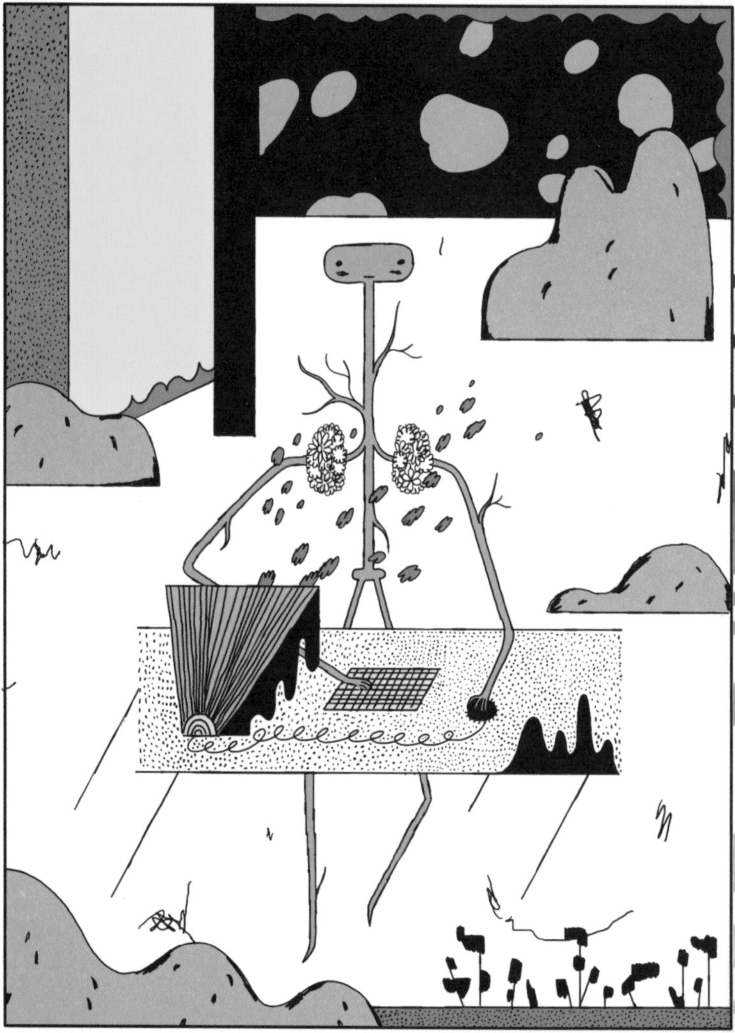

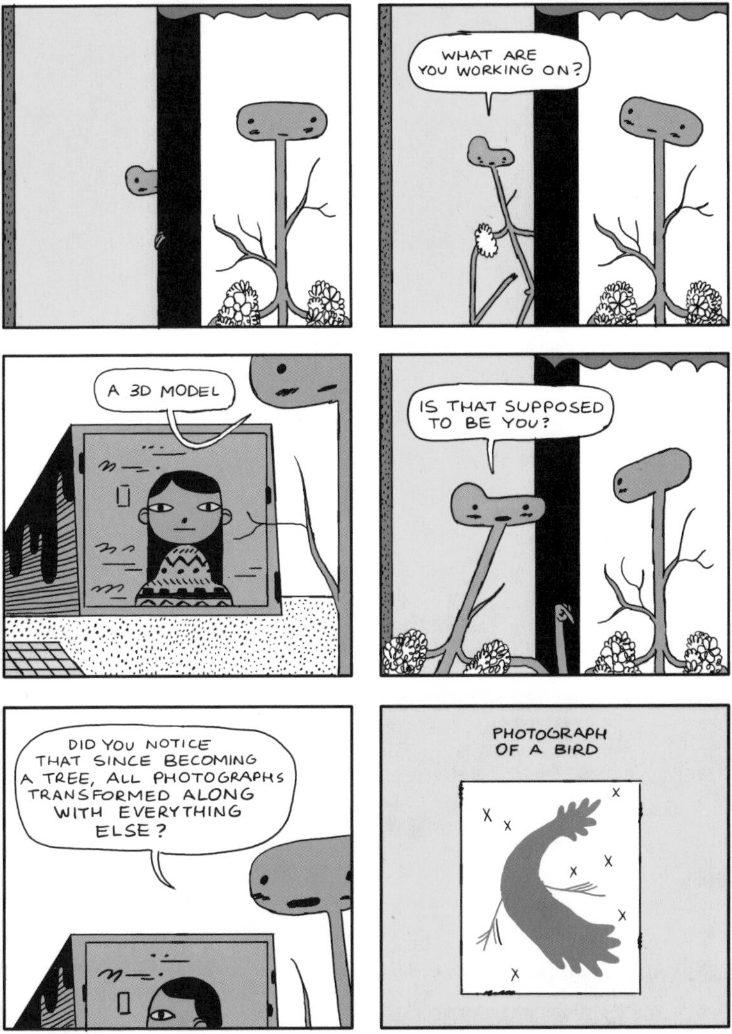
WHAT ARE YOU WORKING ON?
A 3D MODEL
IS THAT SUPPOSED TO BE YOU?
DID YOU NOTICE THAT SINCE BECOMING A TREE, ALL PHOTOGRAPHS TRANSFORMED ALONG WITH EVERYTHING ELSE?
PHOTOGRAPH OF A BIRD

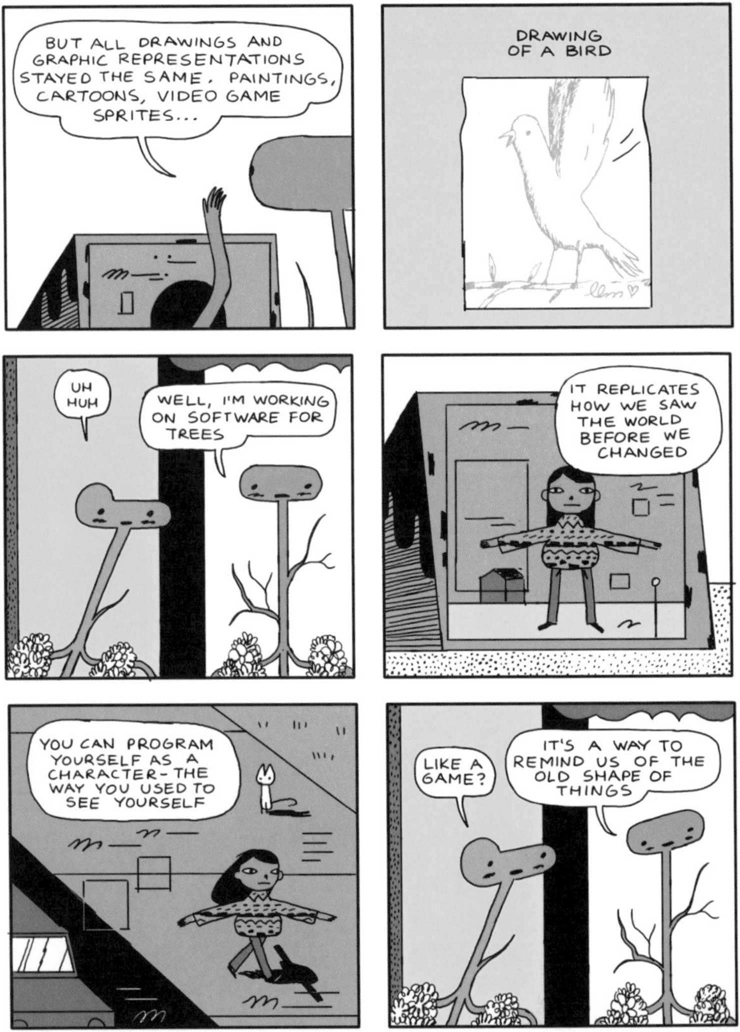
BUT ALL DRAWINGS AND GRAPHIC REPRESENTATIONS STAYED THE SAME. PAINTINGS, CARTOONS, VIDEO GAME SPRITES...
DRAWING OF A BIRD
UH HUH
WELL, I'M WORKING ON SOFTWARE FOR TREES
IT REPLICATES HOW WE SAW THE WORLD BEFORE WE CHANGED
YOU CAN PROGRAM YOURSELF AS A CHARACTER- THE WAY YOU USED TO SEE YOURSELF
LIKE A GAME?
IT'S A WAY TO REMIND US OF THE OLD SHAPE OF THINGS

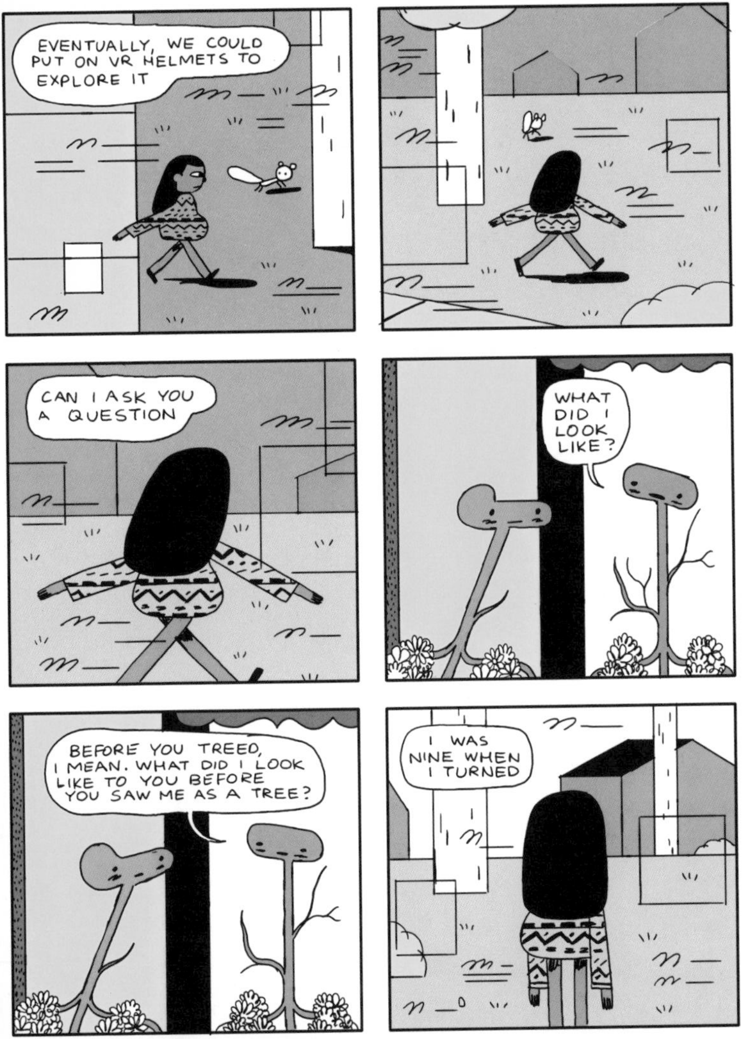
EVENTUALLY, WE COULD PUT ON VR HELMETS TO EXPLORE IT
CAN I ASK YOU A QUESTION
WHAT DID I LOOK LIKE?
BEFORE YOU TREED, I MEAN. WHAT DID I LOOK LIKE TO YOU BEFORE YOU SAW ME AS A TREE?
I WAS NINE WHEN I TURNED

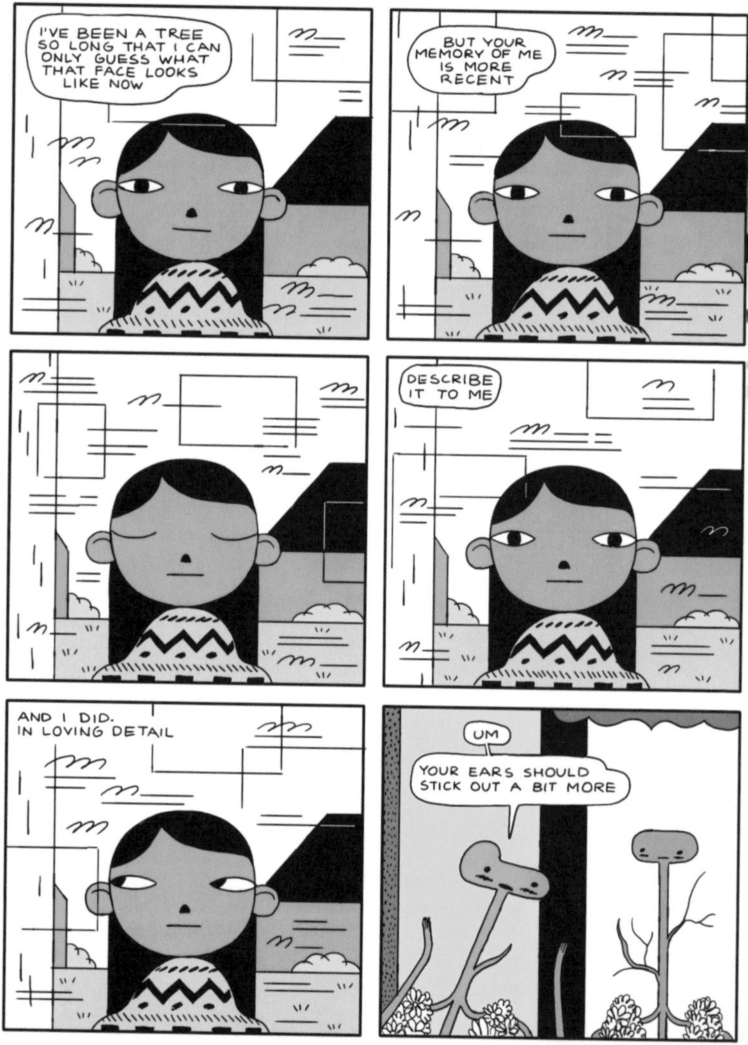
I'VE BEEN A TREE SO LONG THAT I CAN ONLY GUESS WHAT THAT FACE LOOKS LIKE NOW
BUT YOUR MEMORY OF ME IS MORE RECENT
DESCRIBE IT TO ME
AND I DID. IN LOVING DETAIL
UM
YOUR EARS SHOULD STICK OUT A BIT MORE

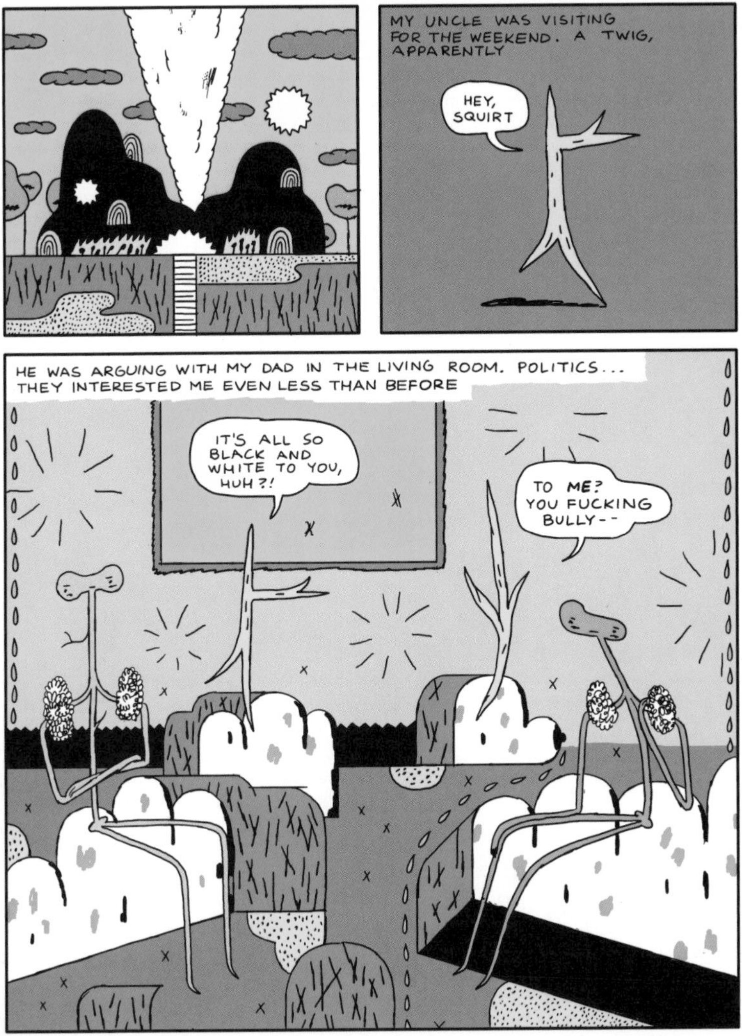
MY UNCLE WAS VISITING FOR THE WEEKEND. A TWIG, APPARENTLY
HEY, SQUIRT
HE WAS ARGUING WITH MY DAD IN THE LIVING ROOM. POLITICS... THEY INTERESTED ME EVEN LESS THAN BEFORE
IT'S ALL SO BLACK AND WHITE TO YOU, HUH?!
TO ME? YOU FUCKING BULLY--

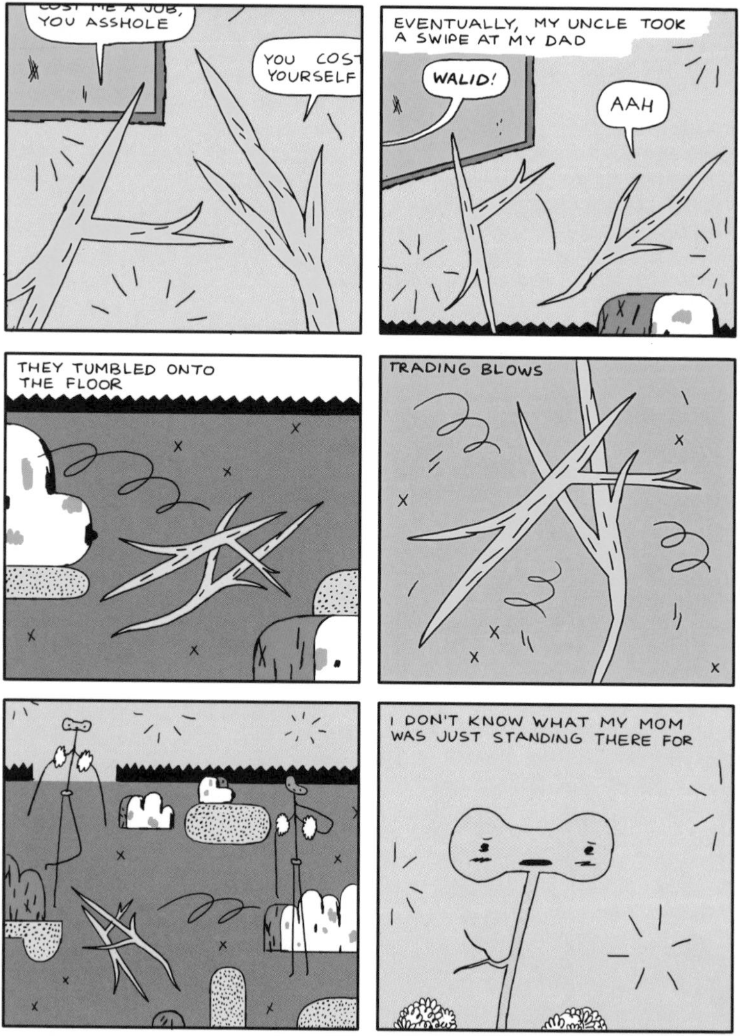
YOU ASSHOLE
YOU COST YOURSELF
EVENTUALLY, MY UNCLE TOOK A SWIPE AT MY DAD
WALID!
AAH
THEY TUMBLED ONTO THE FLOOR
TRADING BLOWS
I DON'T KNOW WHAT MY MOM WAS JUST STANDING THERE FOR

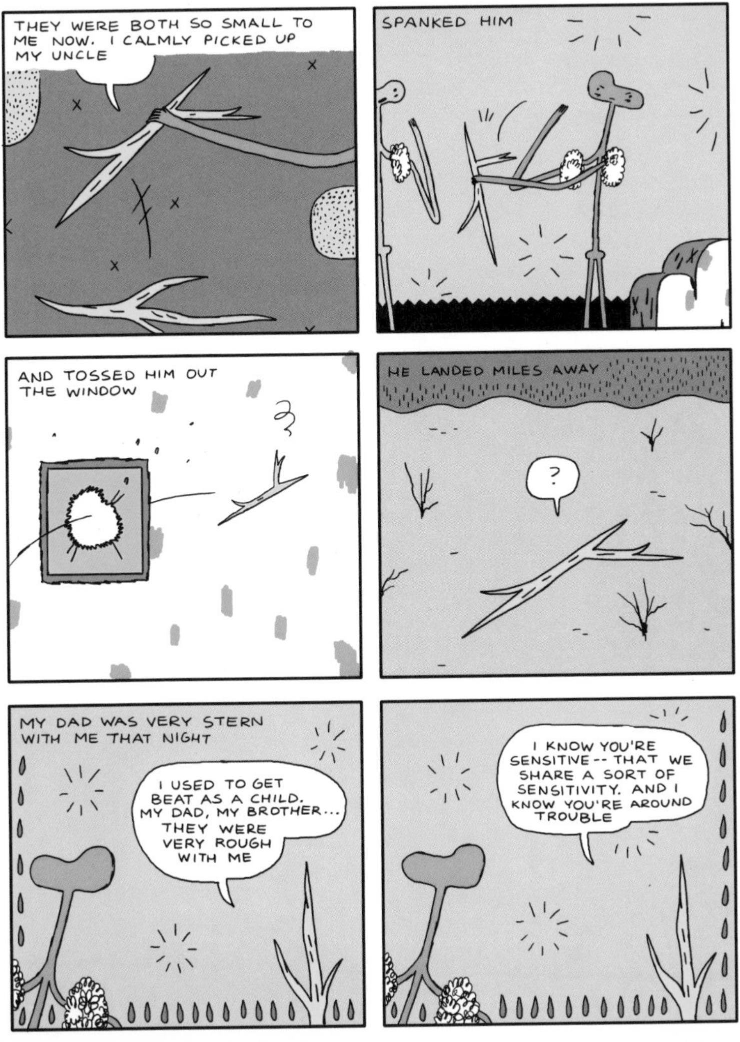
THEY WERE BOTH SO SMALL TO ME NOW. I CALMLY PICKED UP MY UNCLE
SPANKED HIM
AND TOSSED HIM OUT THE WINDOW
HE LANDED MILES AWAY
?
MY DAD WAS VERY STERN WITH ME THAT NIGHT
I USED TO GET BEAT AS A CHILD. MY DAD, MY BROTHER... THEY WERE VERY ROUGH WITH ME
I KNOW YOU'RE SENSITIVE -- THAT WE SHARE A SORT OF SENSITIVITY. AND I KNOW YOU'RE AROUND TROUBLE

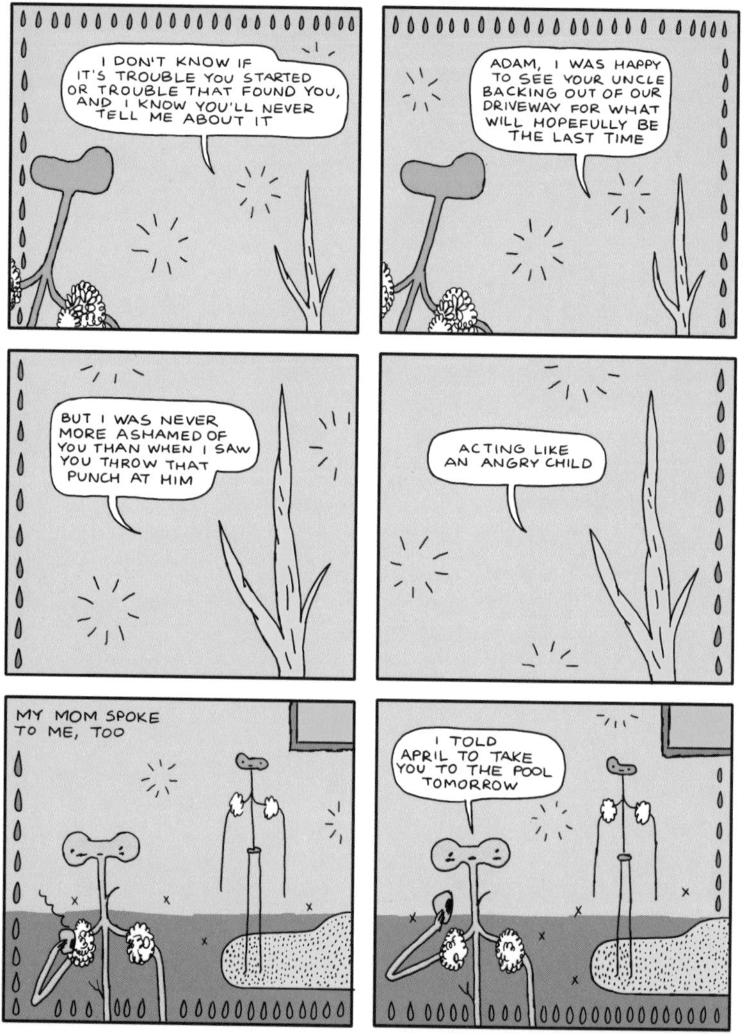
I DON'T KNOW IF IT'S TROUBLE YOU STARTED OR TROUBLE THAT FOUND YOU, AND I KNOW YOU'LL NEVER TELL ME ABOUT IT
ADAM, I WAS HAPPY TO SEE YOUR UNCLE BACKING OUT OF OUR DRIVEWAY FOR WHAT WILL HOPEFULLY BE THE LAST TIME
BUT I WAS NEVER MORE ASHAMED OF YOU THAN WHEN I SAW YOU THROW THAT PUNCH AT HIM
ACTING LIKE AN ANGRY CHILD
MY MOM SPOKE TO ME, TOO
I TOLD APRIL TO TAKE YOU TO THE POOL TOMORROW

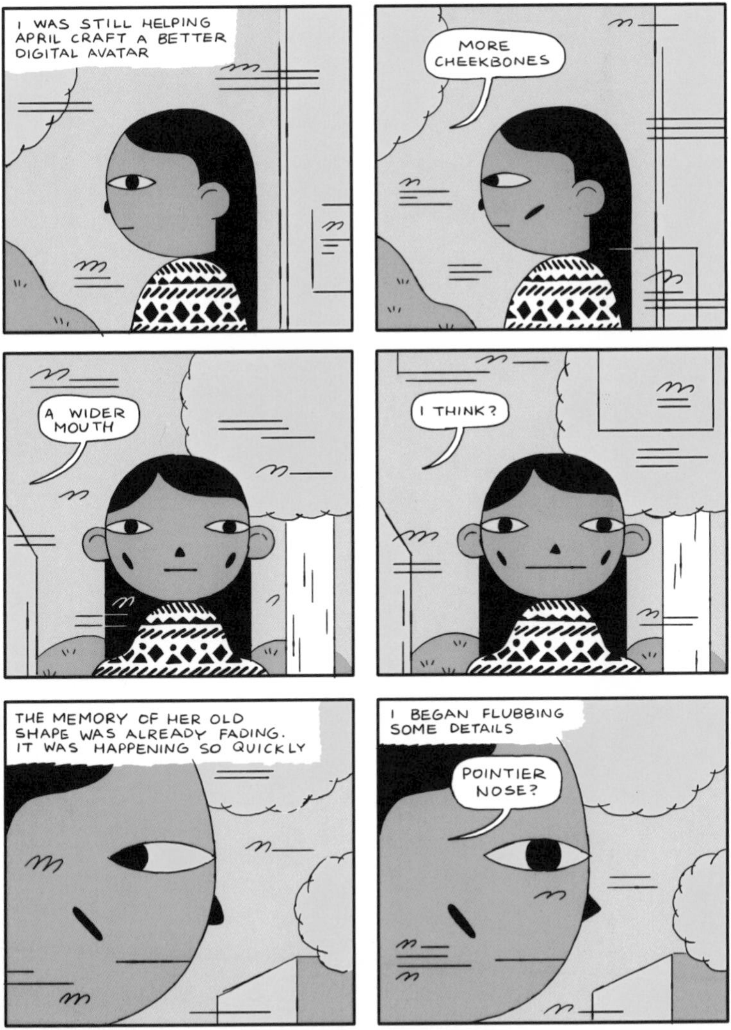
I WAS STILL HELPING APRIL CRAFT A BETTER DIGITAL AVATAR
MORE CHEEKBONES
A WIDER MOUTH
I THINK?
THE MEMORY OF HER OLD SHAPE WAS ALREADY FADING. IT WAS HAPPENING SO QUICKLY
I BEGAN FLUBBING SOME DETAILS
POINTIER NOSE?

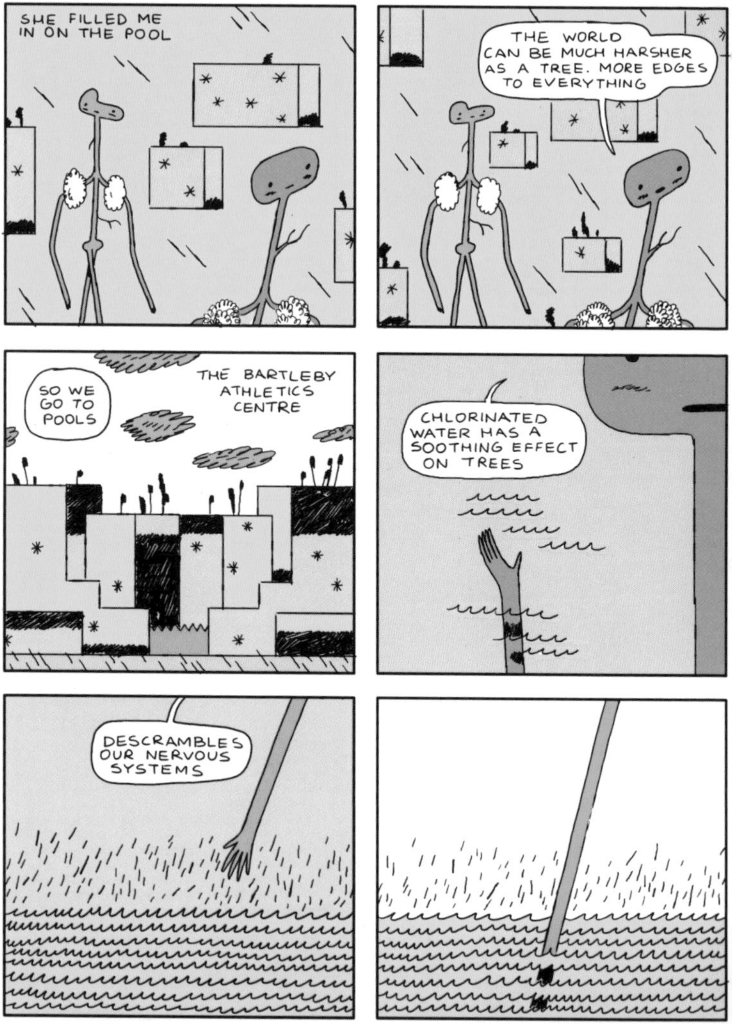
SHE FILLED ME IN ON THE POOL
THE WORLD CAN BE MUCH HARSHER AS A TREE. MORE EDGES TO EVERYTHING
SO WE GO TO POOLS
THE BARTLEBY ATHLETICS CENTRE
CHLORINATED WATER HAS A SOOTHING EFFECT ON TREES
DESCRAMBLES OUR NERVOUS SYSTEMS

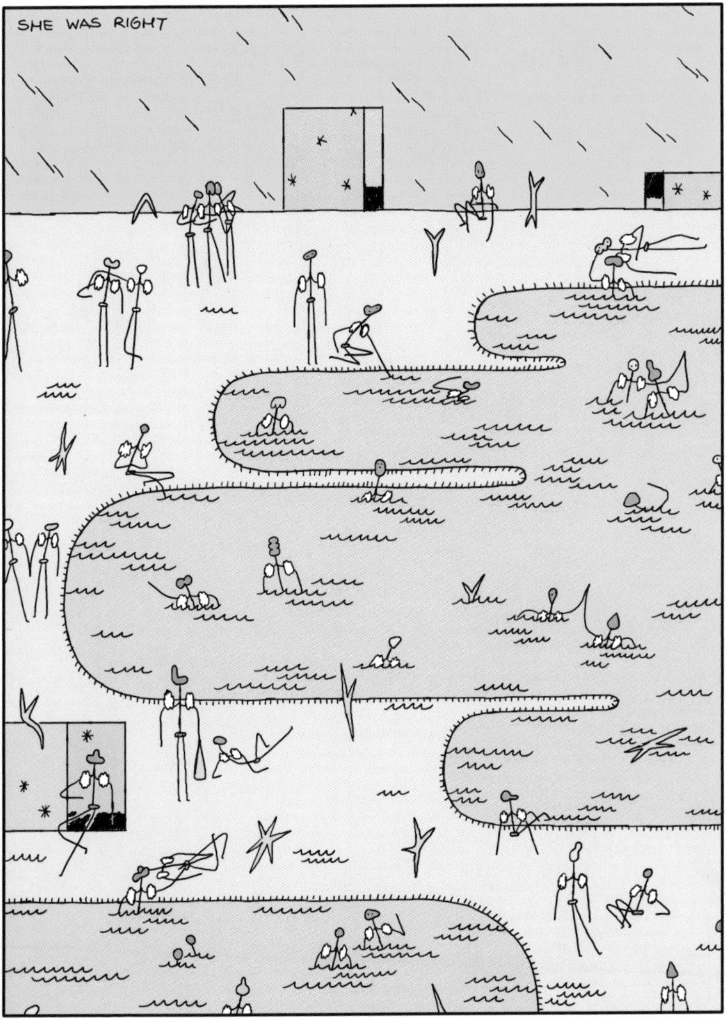
SHE WAS RIGHT

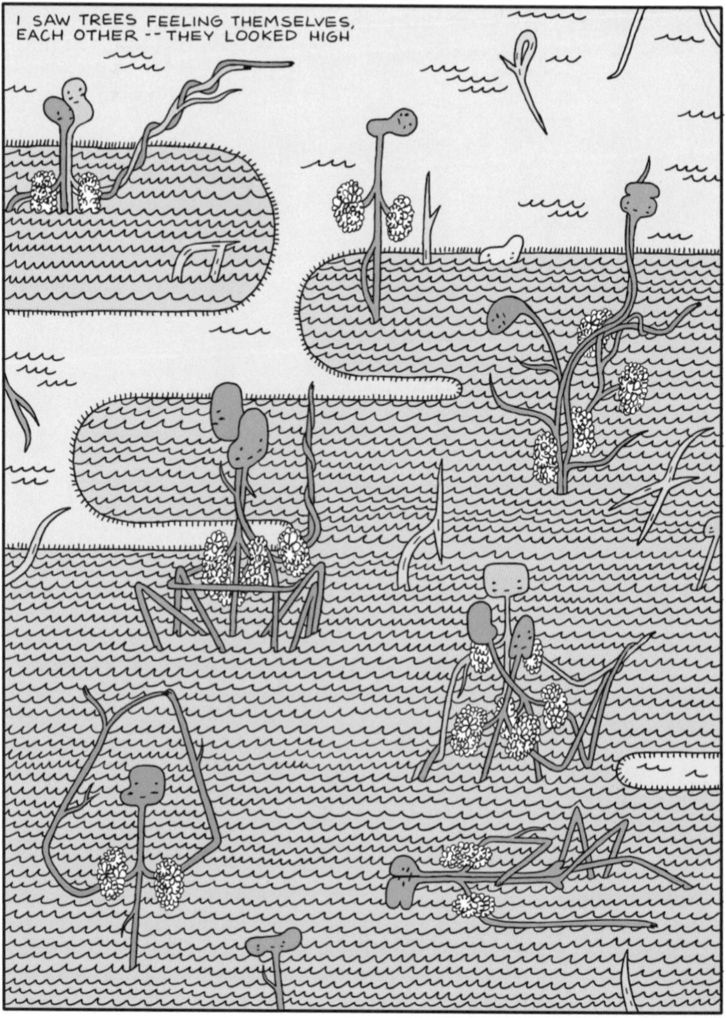
I SAW TREES FEELING THEMSELVES, EACH OTHER -- THEY LOOKED HIGH

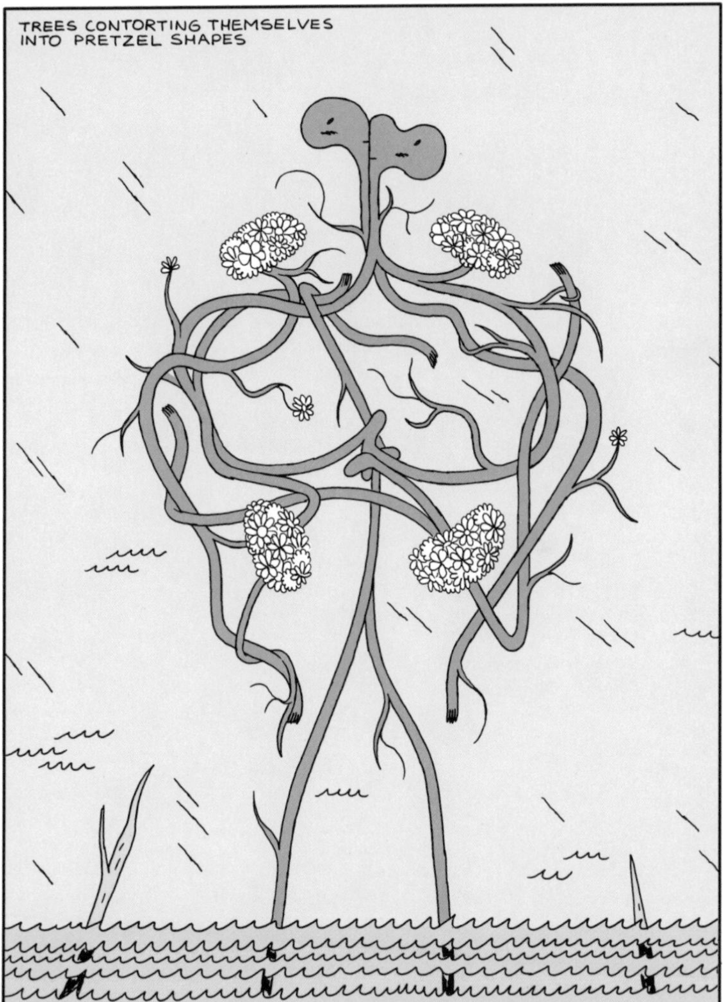
TREES CONTORTING THEMSELVES
INTO PRETZEL SHAPES

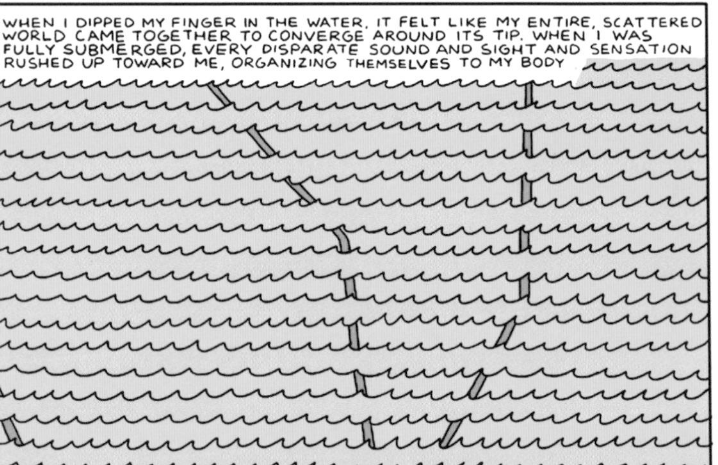
WHEN I DIPPED MY FINGER IN THE WATER, IT FELT LIKE MY ENTIRE, SCATTERED WORLD CAME TOGETHER TO CONVERGE AROUND ITS TIP. WHEN I WAS FULLY SUBMERGED, EVERY DISPARATE SOUND AND SIGHT AND SENSATION RUSHED UP TOWARD ME, ORGANIZING THEMSELVES TO MY BODY

I HAD NO IDEA OUR BODIES COULD DO THIS
MM HMM
WON'T THE TWIGS IN THE POOL NOTICE US? WHAT DO WE LOOK LIKE TO THEM
THEY CAN'T TELL. I THINK THEY JUST SEE US SPLASHING AROUND OR SOMETHING

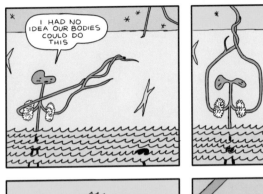

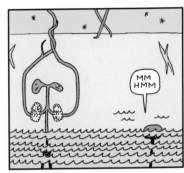

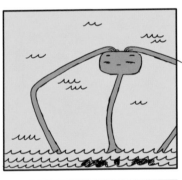

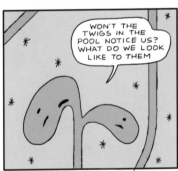

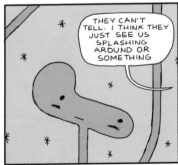

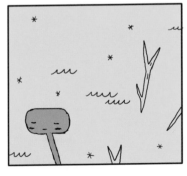

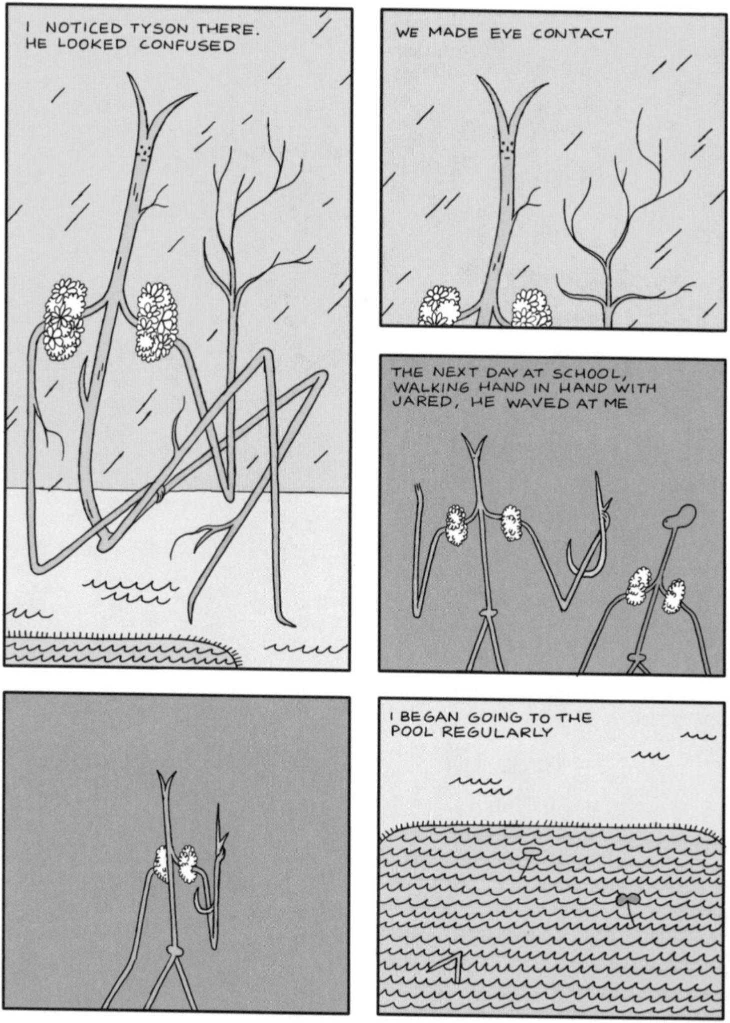
I NOTICED TYSON THERE. HE LOOKED CONFUSED
WE MADE EYE CONTACT
THE NEXT DAY AT SCHOOL, WALKING HAND IN HAND WITH JARED, HE WAVED AT ME
I BEGAN GOING TO THE POOL REGULARLY

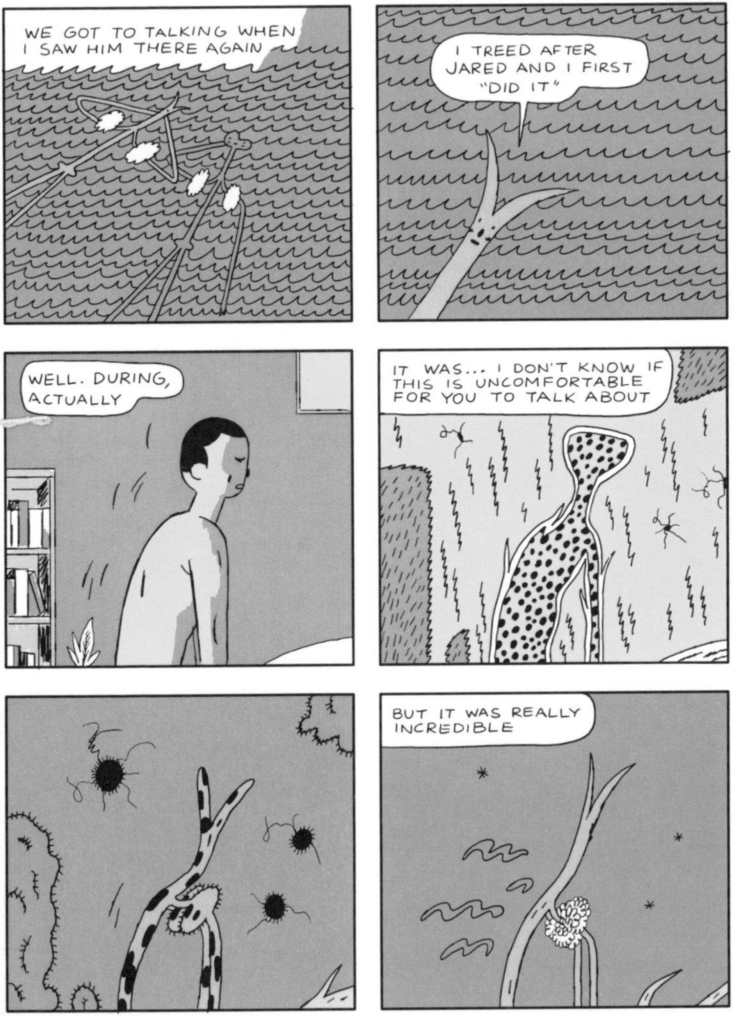
WE GOT TO TALKING WHEN I SAW HIM THERE AGAIN
I TREED AFTER JARED AND I FIRST "DID IT"
WELL. DURING, ACTUALLY
IT WAS... I DON'T KNOW IF THIS IS UNCOMFORTABLE FOR YOU TO TALK ABOUT
BUT IT WAS REALLY INCREDIBLE

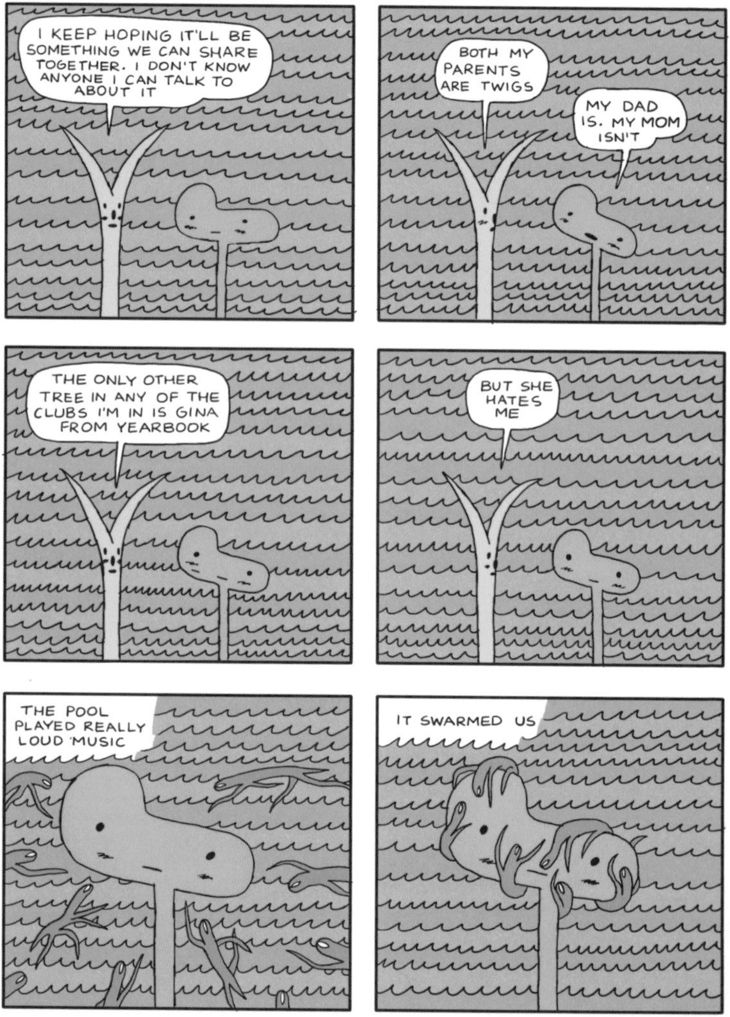
I KEEP HOPING IT'LL BE SOMETHING WE CAN SHARE TOGETHER. I DON'T KNOW ANYONE I CAN TALK TO ABOUT IT
BOTH MY PARENTS ARE TWIGS
MY DAD IS. MY MOM ISN'T
THE ONLY OTHER TREE IN ANY OF THE CLUBS I'M IN IS GINA FROM YEARBOOK
BUT SHE HATES ME
THE POOL PLAYED REALLY LOUD MUSIC
IT SWARMED US

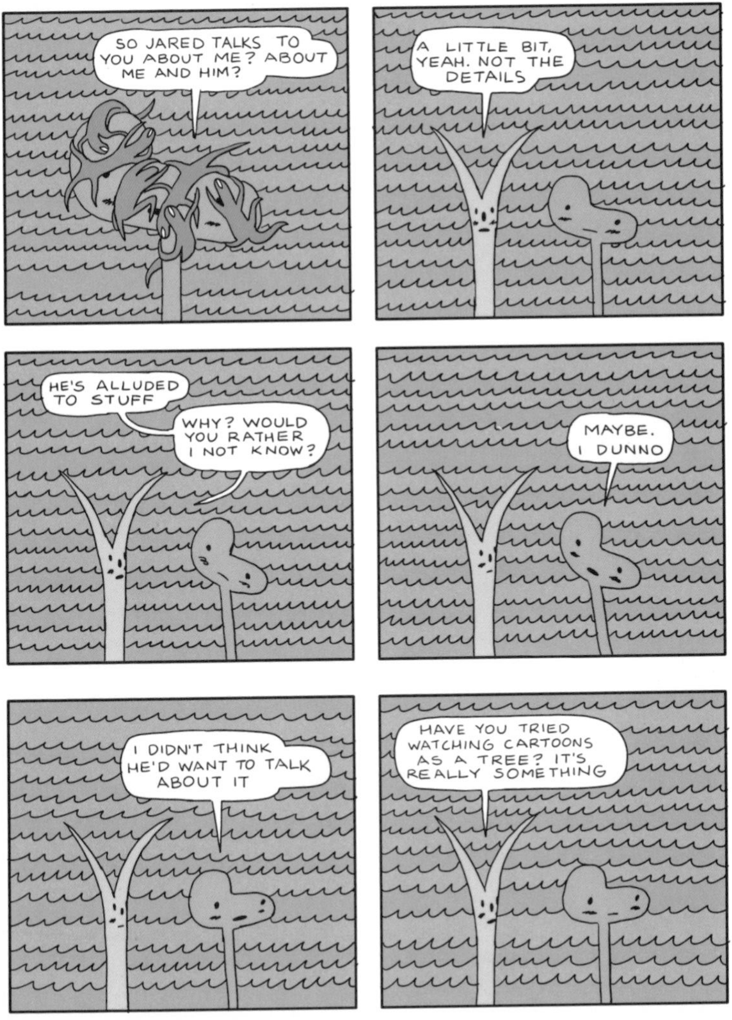

SO JARED TALKS TO YOU ABOUT ME? ABOUT ME AND HIM?
A LITTLE BIT, YEAH. NOT THE DETAILS
HE'S ALLUDED TO STUFF
WHY? WOULD YOU RATHER I NOT KNOW?
MAYBE. I DUNNO
I DIDN'T THINK HE'D WANT TO TALK ABOUT IT
HAVE YOU TRIED WATCHING CARTOONS AS A TREE? IT'S REALLY SOMETHING

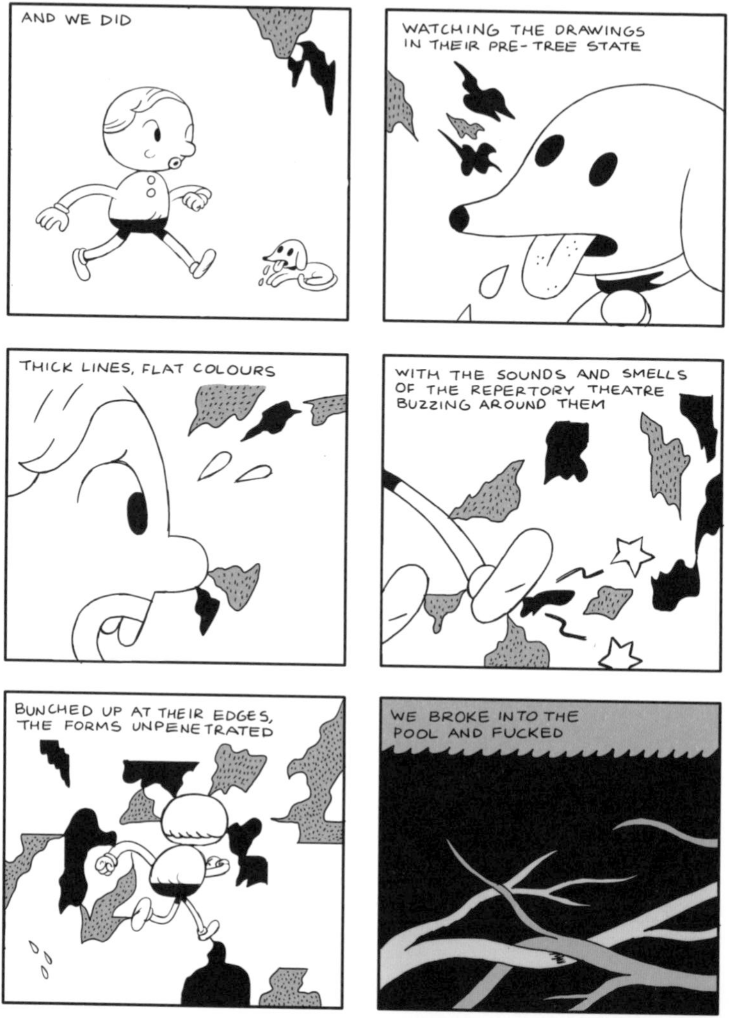
AND WE DID
WATCHING THE DRAWINGS IN THEIR PRE-TREE STATE
THICK LINES, FLAT COLOURS
WITH THE SOUNDS AND SMELLS OF THE REPERTORY THEATRE BUZZING AROUND THEM
BUNCHED UP AT THEIR EDGES, THE FORMS UNPENETRATED
WE BROKE INTO THE POOL AND FUCKED

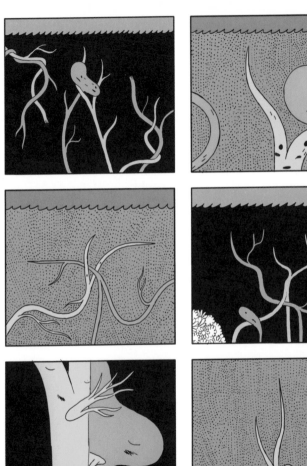
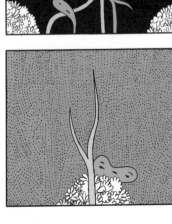

AS IT WAS HAPPENING, I TRIED TO RECALL WHAT BEING WITH JARED WAS LIKE

RUBBING THAT STICKY SHIT HE'D PUT IN HIS HAIR OFF MY PALMS

THE FURROW IN HIS BROW

BUT THE IMAGES WOULDN'T STAY PUT

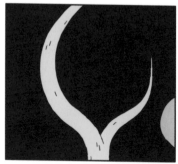

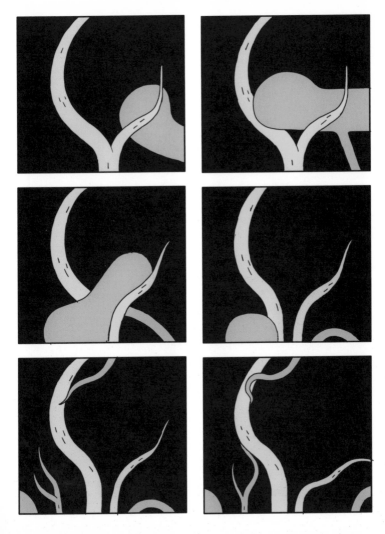

HE COULDN'T MAKE ME COME, BUT I DIDN'T MIND

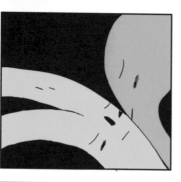

I EVENTUALLY WENT SOFT AND WASN'T EMBARRASSED

WE HUGGED

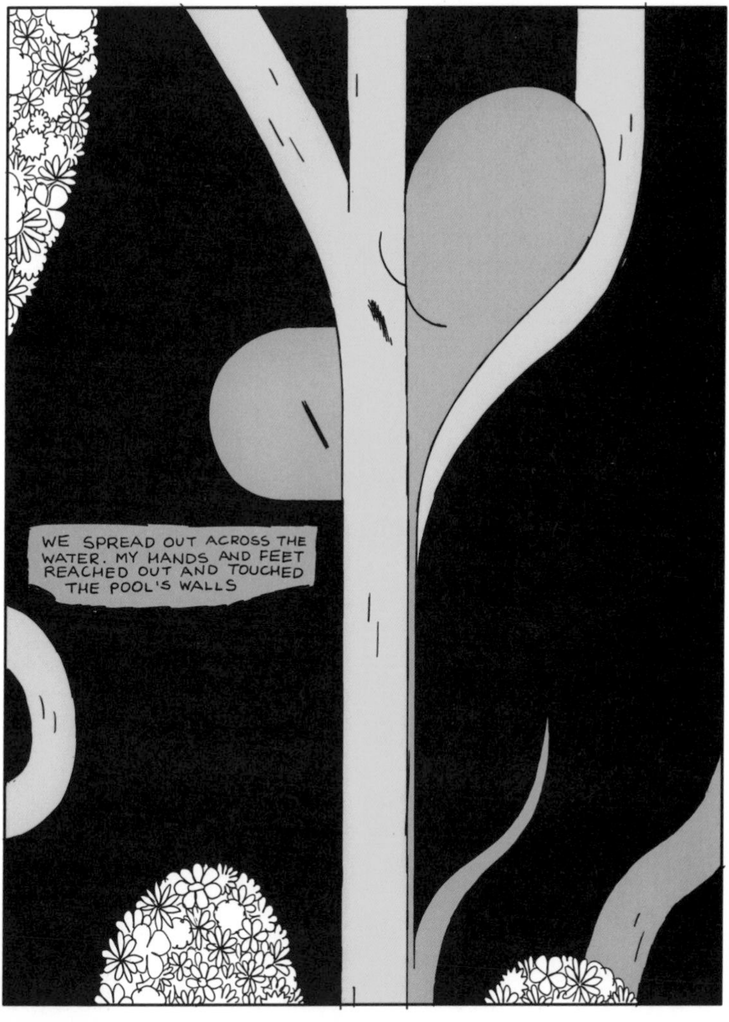
WE SPREAD OUT ACROSS THE WATER. MY HANDS AND FEET REACHED OUT AND TOUCHED THE POOL'S WALLS

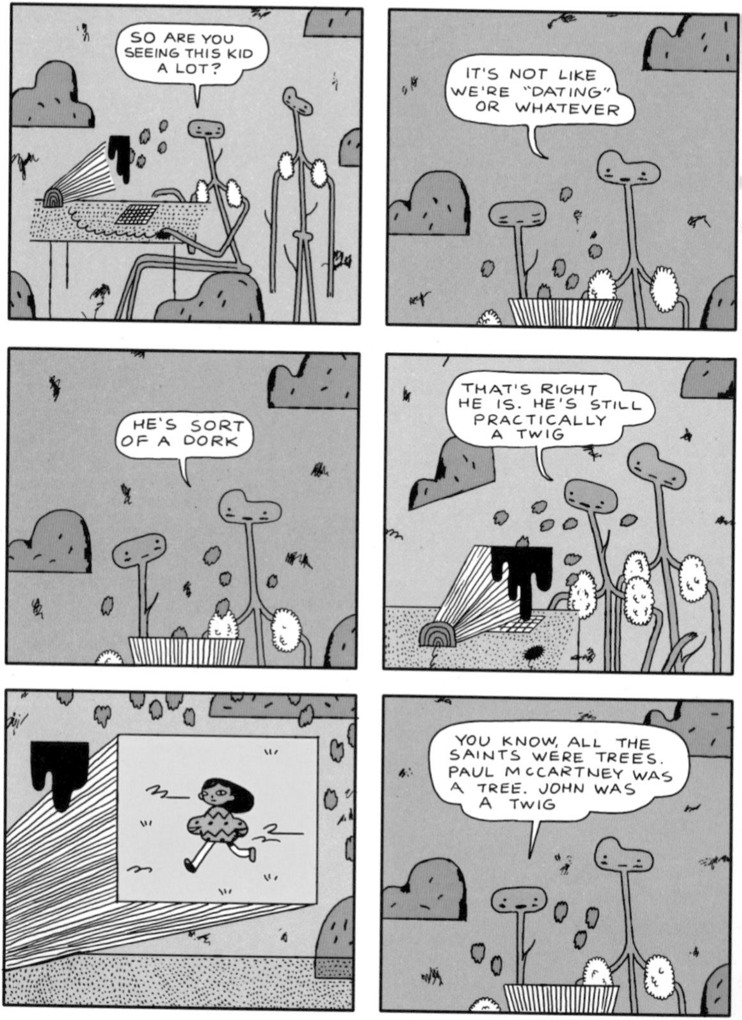
SO ARE YOU SEEING THIS KID A LOT?
IT'S NOT LIKE WE'RE "DATING" OR WHATEVER
HE'S SORT OF A DORK
THAT'S RIGHT HE IS. HE'S STILL PRACTICALLY A TWIG
YOU KNOW, ALL THE SAINTS WERE TREES. PAUL McCARTNEY WAS A TREE. JOHN WAS A TWIG

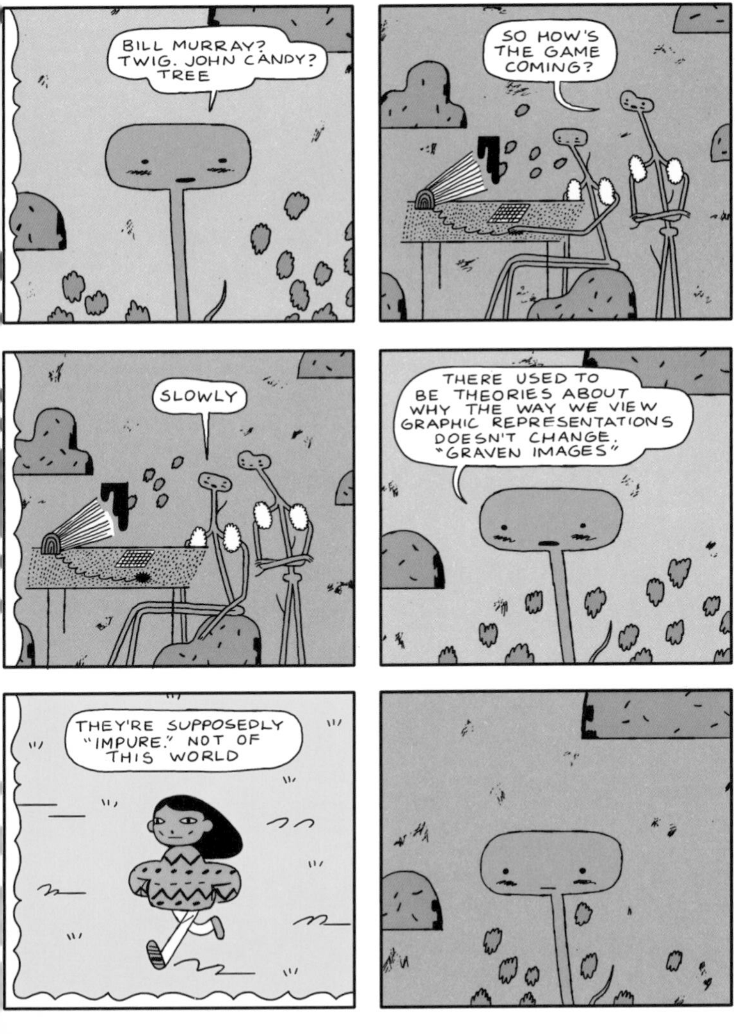

BILL MURRAY? TWIG. JOHN CANDY? TREE
SO HOW'S THE GAME COMING?
SLOWLY
THERE USED TO BE THEORIES ABOUT WHY THE WAY WE VIEW GRAPHIC REPRESENTATIONS DOESN'T CHANGE. "GRAVEN IMAGES"
THEY'RE SUPPOSEDLY "IMPURE." NOT OF THIS WORLD

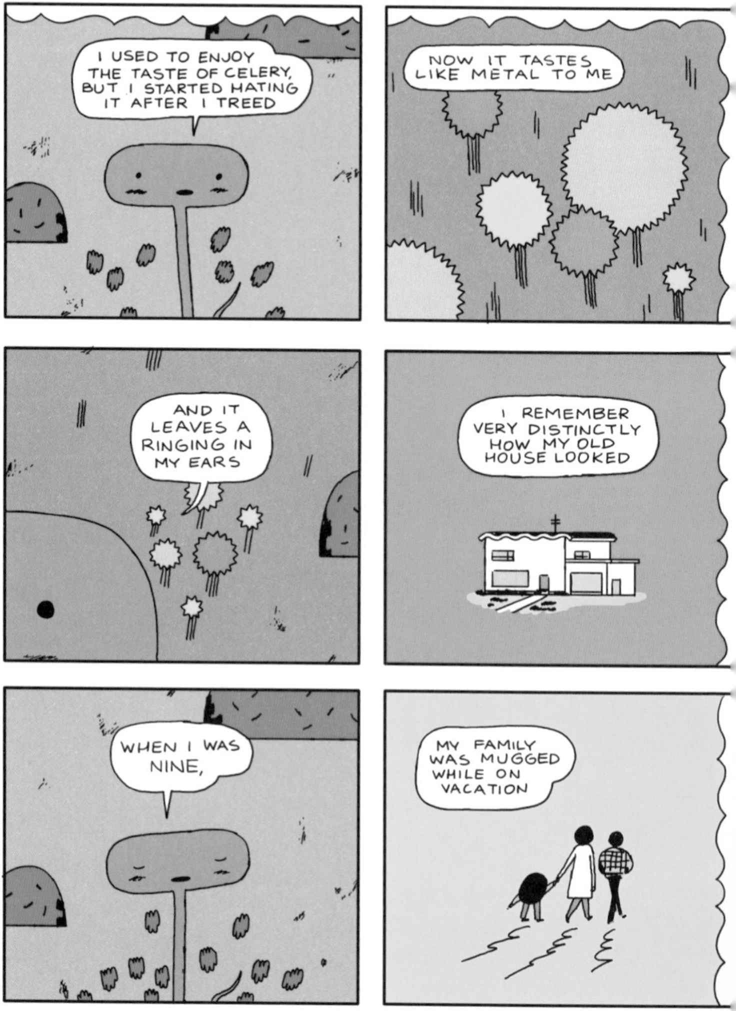
I USED TO ENJOY THE TASTE OF CELERY, BUT I STARTED HATING IT AFTER I TREED
NOW IT TASTES LIKE METAL TO ME
AND IT LEAVES A RINGING IN MY EARS
I REMEMBER VERY DISTINCTLY HOW MY OLD HOUSE LOOKED
WHEN I WAS NINE,
MY FAMILY WAS MUGGED WHILE ON VACATION

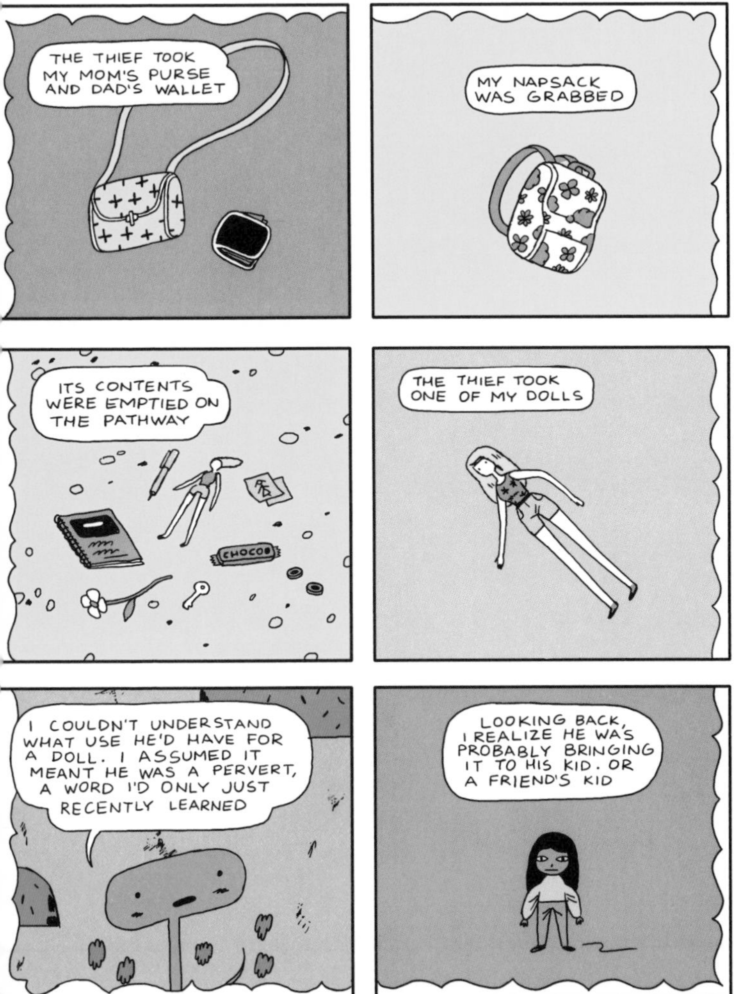
THE THIEF TOOK MY MOM'S PURSE AND DAD'S WALLET
MY NAPSACK WAS GRABBED
ITS CONTENTS WERE EMPTIED ON THE PATHWAY
CHOCOS
THE THIEF TOOK ONE OF MY DOLLS
I COULDN'T UNDERSTAND WHAT USE HE'D HAVE FOR A DOLL. I ASSUMED IT MEANT HE WAS A PERVERT, A WORD I'D ONLY JUST RECENTLY LEARNED
LOOKING BACK, I REALIZE HE WAS PROBABLY BRINGING IT TO HIS KID. OR A FRIEND'S KID

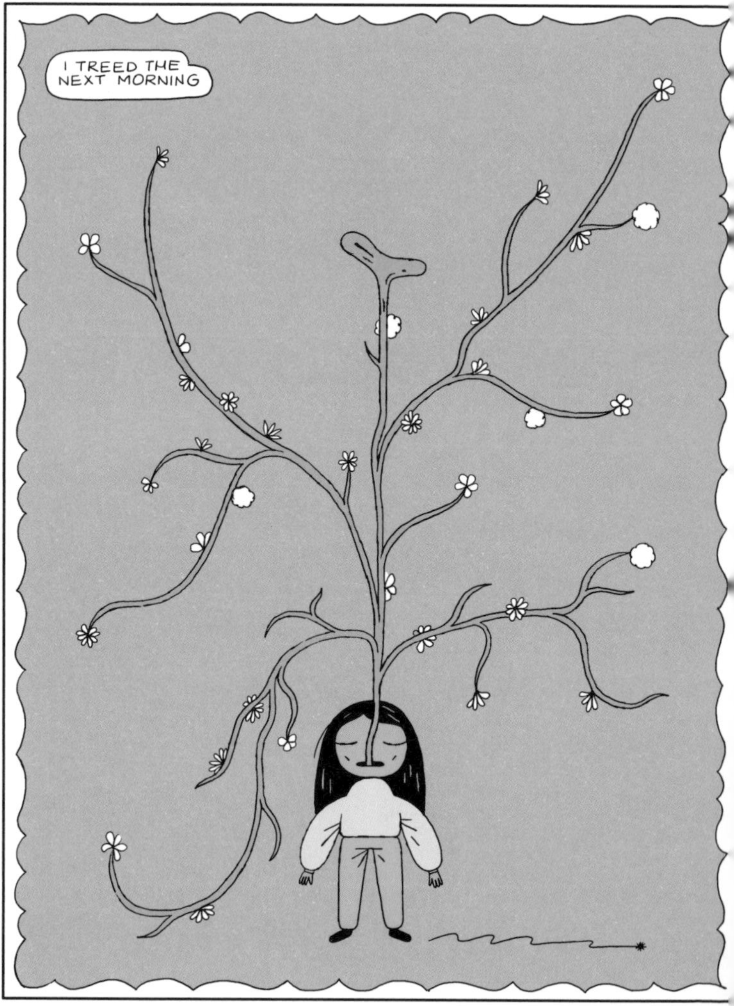
I TREED THE NEXT MORNING

TYSON BROKE UP
WITH JARED
THAT WEEK

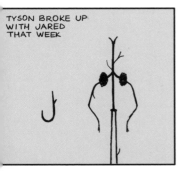

WE HUNG OUT MORE
AS THE SCHOOL YEAR
WOUND DOWN. I MADE
IT CLEAR WE WEREN'T
"DATING"

AND THAT I DIDN'T
WANT KIDS AT SCHOOL
TO SEE US TOGETHER

I'D HAVE PREFERRED TO NOT
SEE HIM AT ALL, HONESTLY.
BUT I DIDN'T WANT TO, LIKE,
ABANDON HIM...

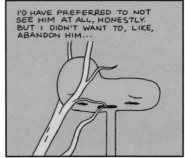

I FELT A SORT OF
RESPONSIBILITY TO HIM

AND THE POOL
STUFF WAS PRETTY
HOT, STILL

WHAT
SCHOOLS ARE
YOU APPLYING
TO?

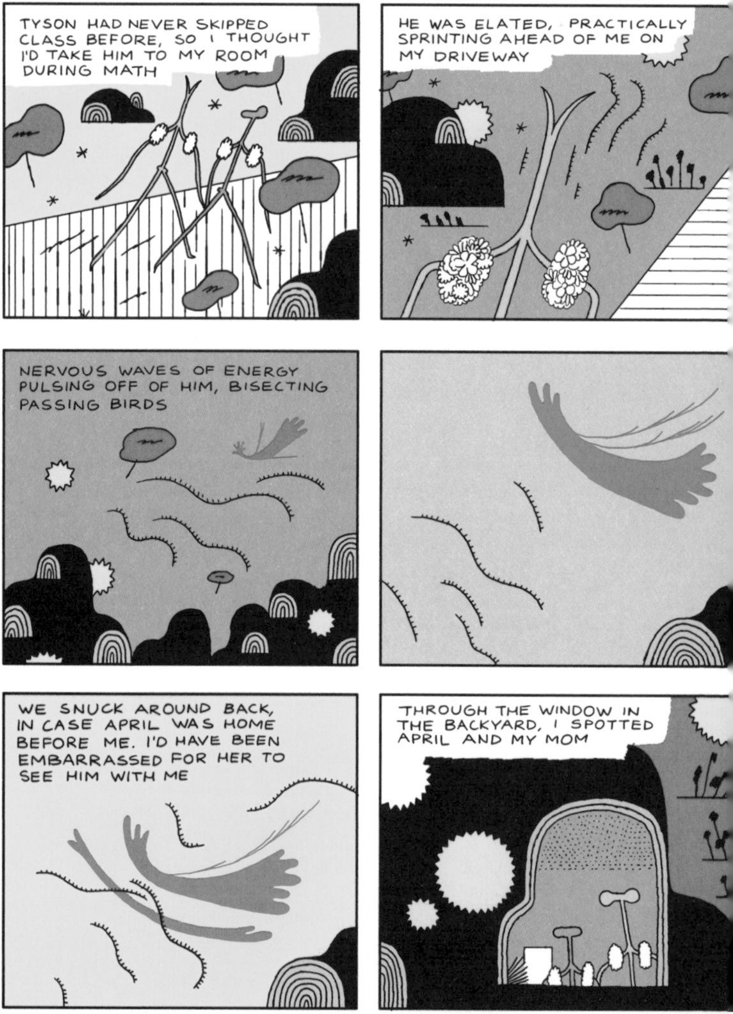
TYSON HAD NEVER SKIPPED CLASS BEFORE, SO I THOUGHT I'D TAKE HIM TO MY ROOM DURING MATH
HE WAS ELATED, PRACTICALLY SPRINTING AHEAD OF ME ON MY DRIVEWAY
NERVOUS WAVES OF ENERGY PULSING OFF OF HIM, BISECTING PASSING BIRDS
WE SNUCK AROUND BACK, IN CASE APRIL WAS HOME BEFORE ME. I'D HAVE BEEN EMBARRASSED FOR HER TO SEE HIM WITH ME
THROUGH THE WINDOW IN THE BACKYARD, I SPOTTED APRIL AND MY MOM

THEY WERE PLAYING APRIL'S GAME.

I COULD SEE OVER MY MOM'S SHOULDER - THERE WAS AN AVATAR OF HER LIKENESS ON THE SCREEN

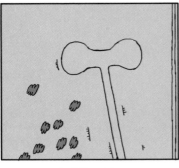

I COULD TELL FROM HER SHAKING, SHE WAS CRYING

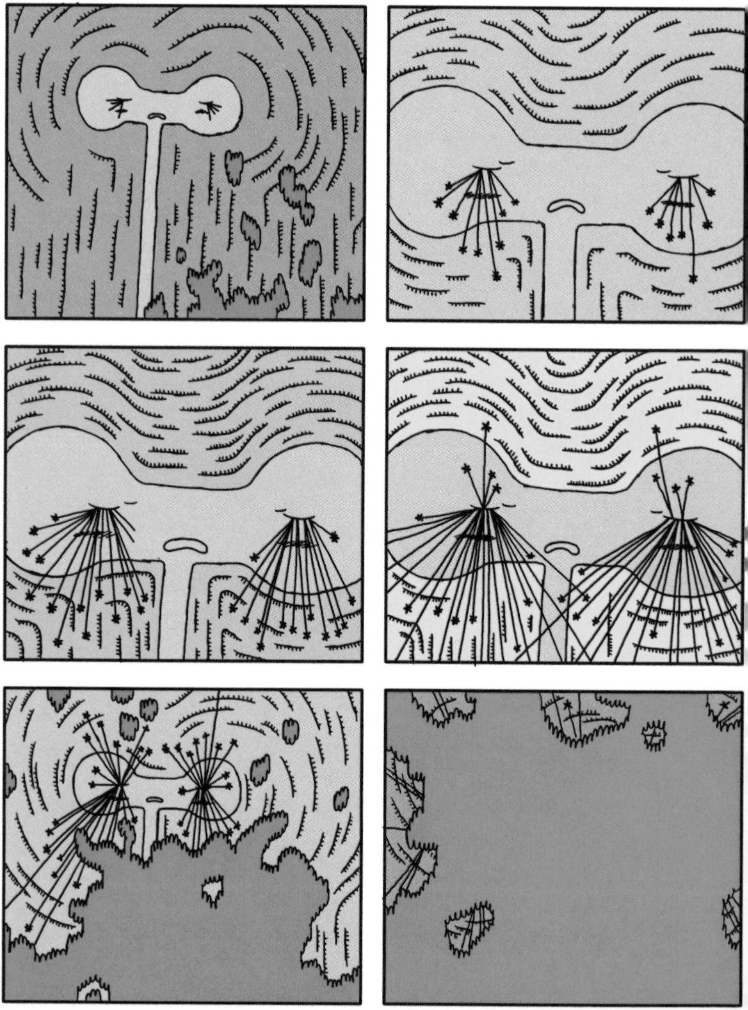

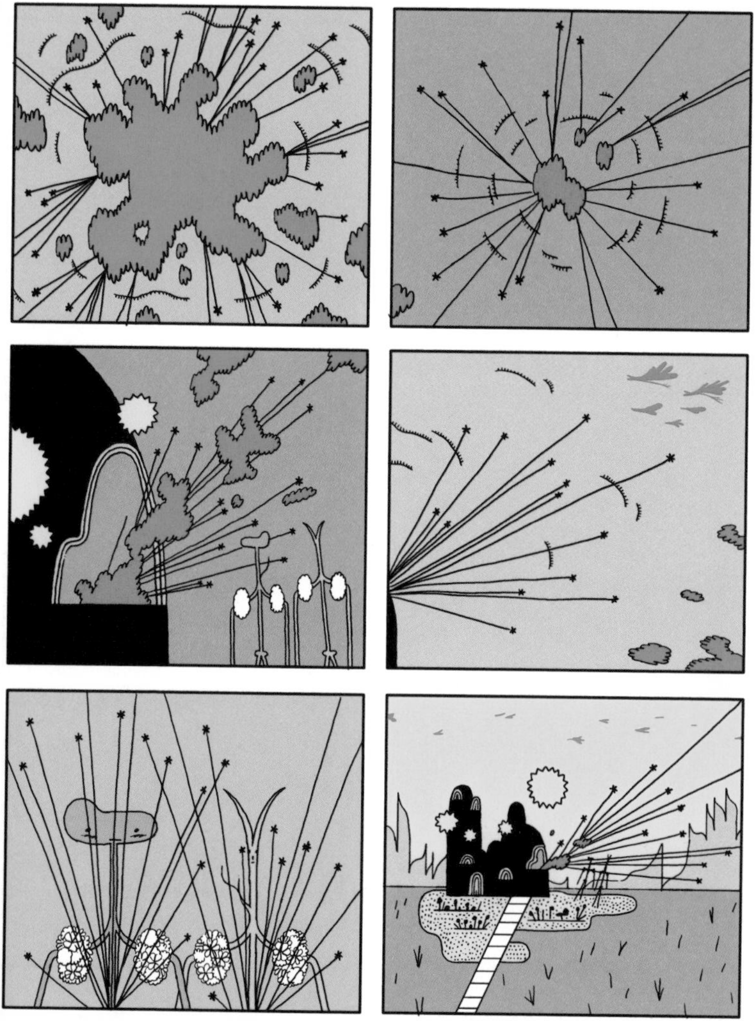

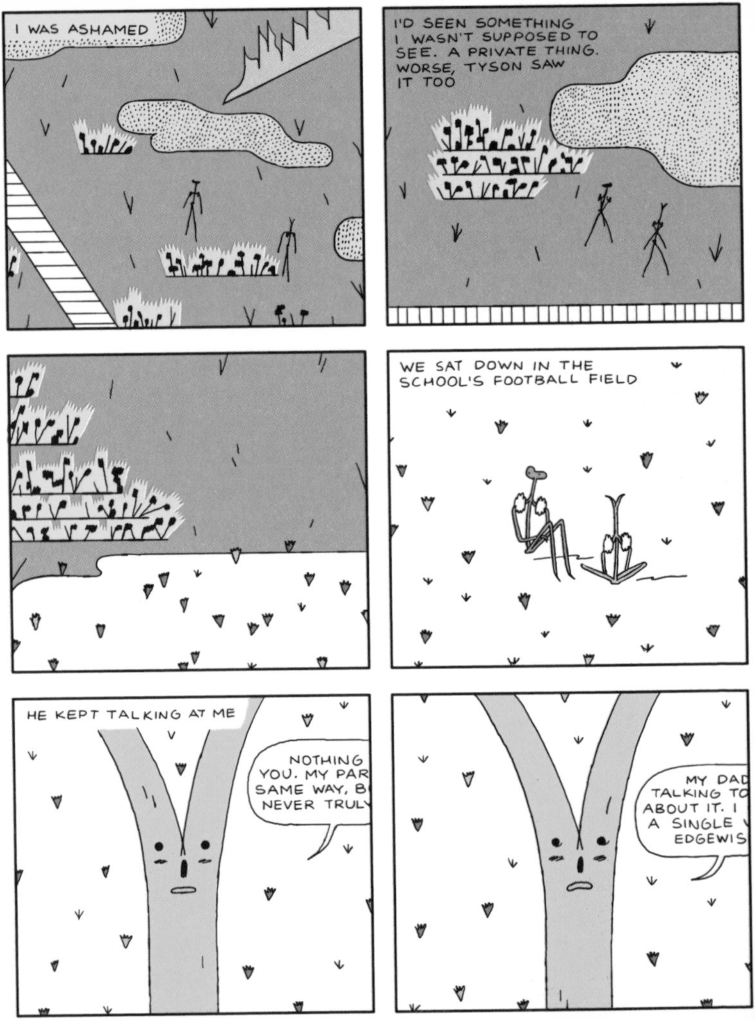
I WAS ASHAMED
I'D SEEN SOMETHING I WASN'T SUPPOSED TO SEE. A PRIVATE THING. WORSE, TYSON SAW IT TOO
WE SAT DOWN IN THE SCHOOL'S FOOTBALL FIELD
HE KEPT TALKING AT ME
NOTHING
YOU. MY PAR
SAME WAY, B
NEVER TRUL
MY DAD
TALKING TO
ABOUT IT. I
A SINGLE
EDGEWIS

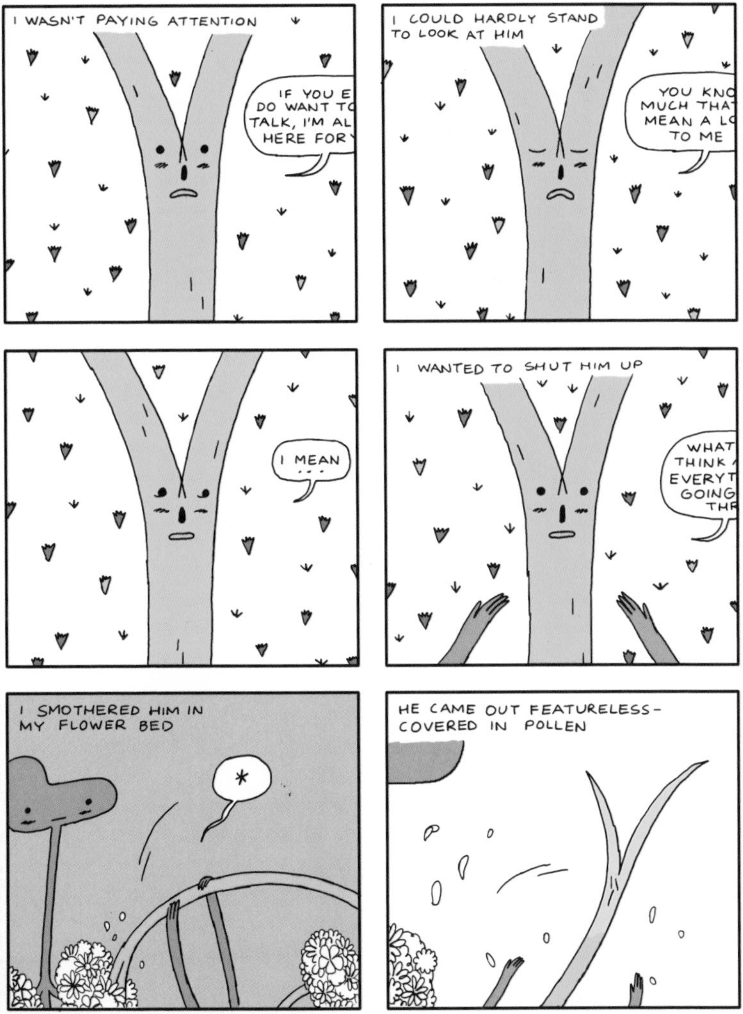
I WASN'T PAYING ATTENTION
IF YOU E DO WANT TO TALK, I'M AL HERE FOR
I COULD HARDLY STAND TO LOOK AT HIM
YOU KNO MUCH THA MEAN A L TO ME
I MEAN ...
I WANTED TO SHUT HIM UP
WHAT THINK EVERYT GOING
I SMOTHERED HIM IN MY FLOWER BED
*
HE CAME OUT FEATURELESS- COVERED IN POLLEN

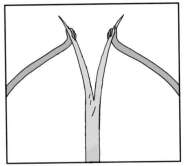

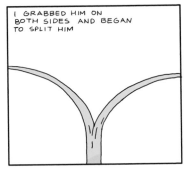

I GRABBED HIM ON BOTH SIDES AND BEGAN TO SPLIT HIM

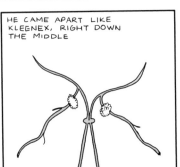

HE CAME APART LIKE KLEENEX, RIGHT DOWN THE MIDDLE

I WORKED ON HIM. PIECE BY PIECE

PLUCKED HIS FOLIAGE

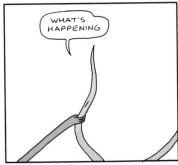

WHAT'S HAPPENING

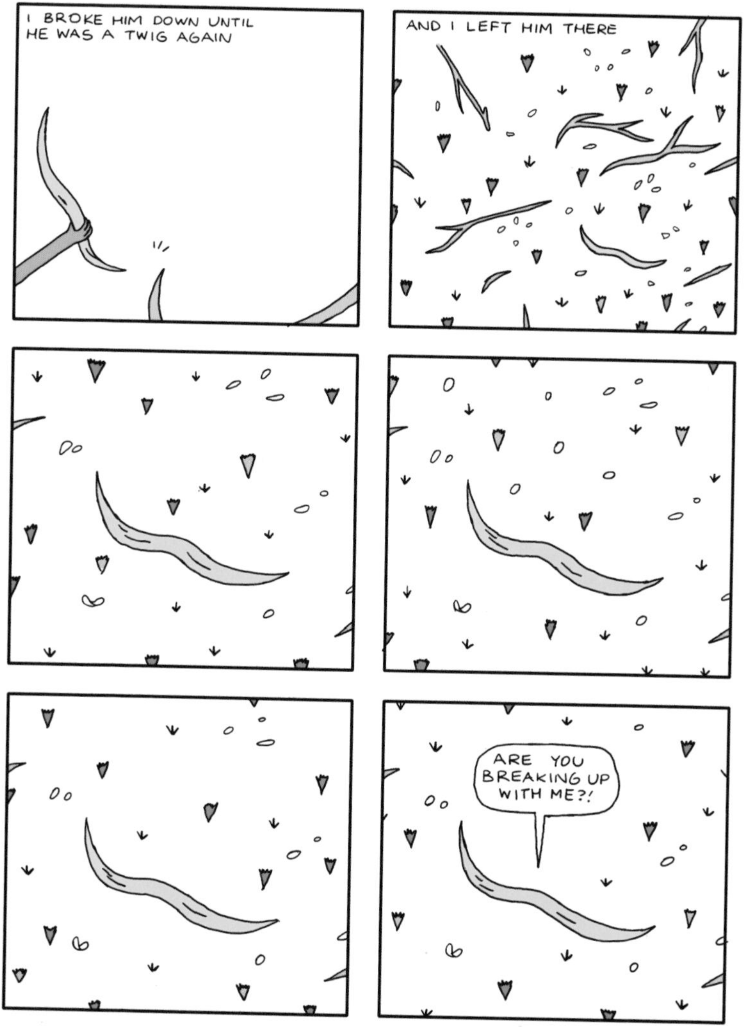
I BROKE HIM DOWN UNTIL HE WAS A TWIG AGAIN
AND I LEFT HIM THERE
ARE YOU BREAKING UP WITH ME?!

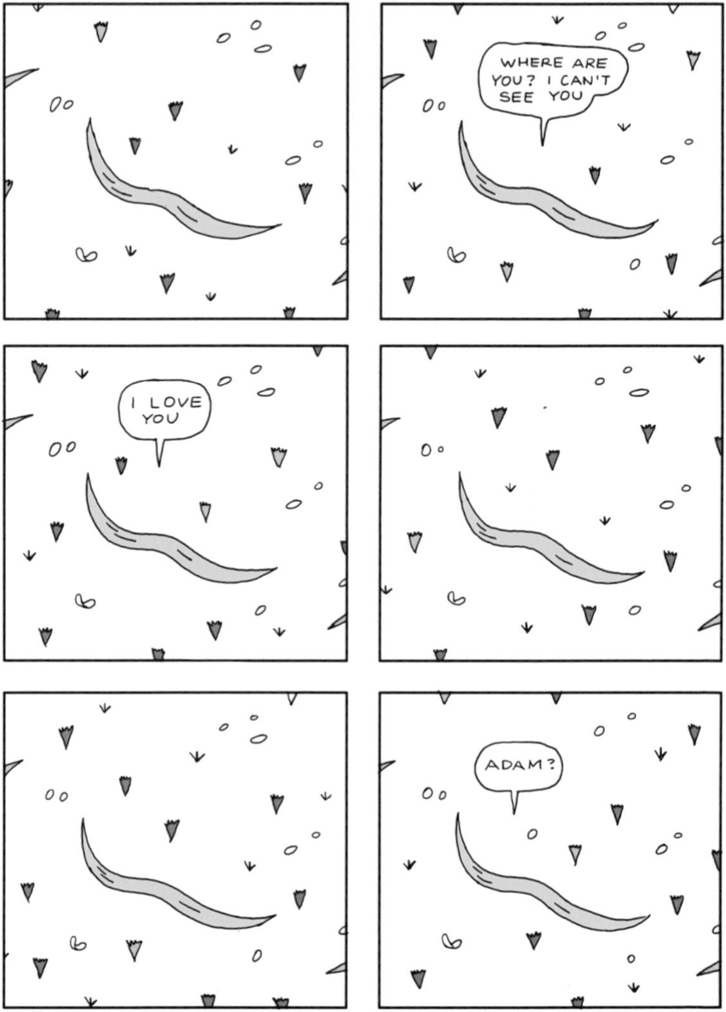
WHERE ARE YOU? I CAN'T SEE YOU
I LOVE YOU
ADAM?

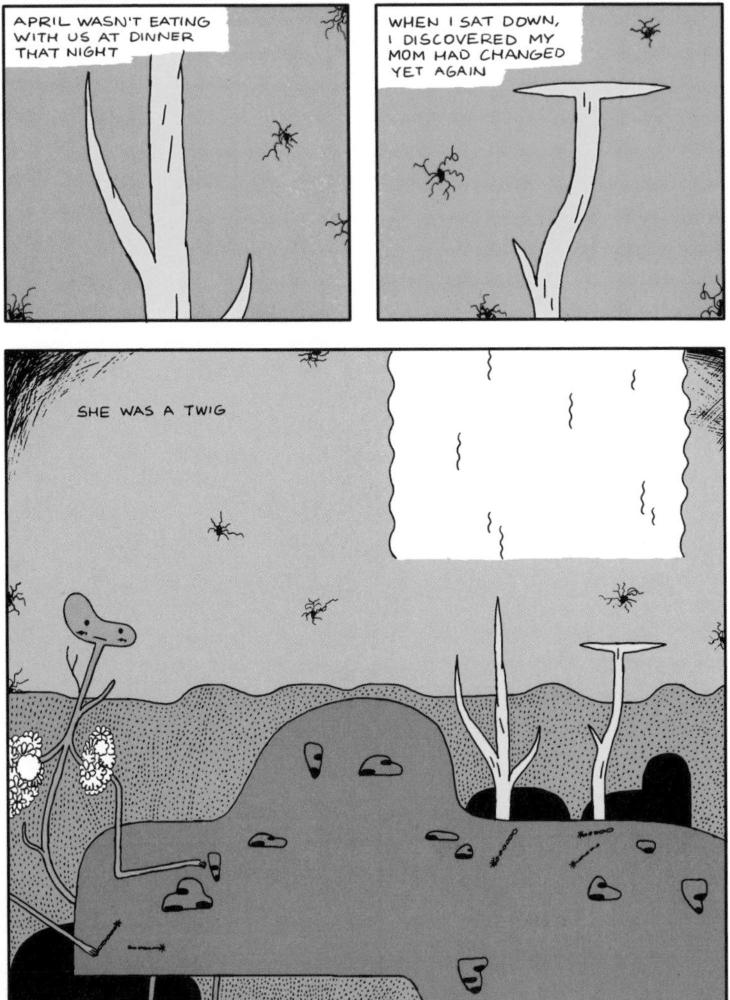
APRIL WASN'T EATING WITH US AT DINNER THAT NIGHT
WHEN I SAT DOWN, I DISCOVERED MY MOM HAD CHANGED YET AGAIN
SHE WAS A TWIG

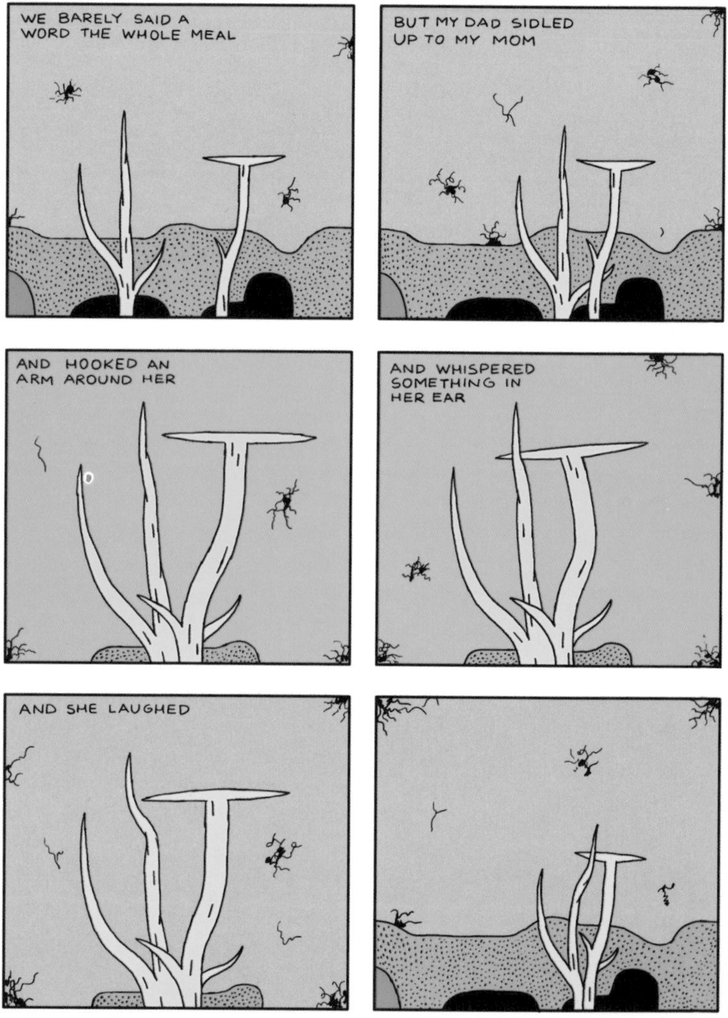
WE BARELY SAID A WORD THE WHOLE MEAL
BUT MY DAD SIDLED UP TO MY MOM
AND HOOKED AN ARM AROUND HER
AND WHISPERED SOMETHING IN HER EAR
AND SHE LAUGHED

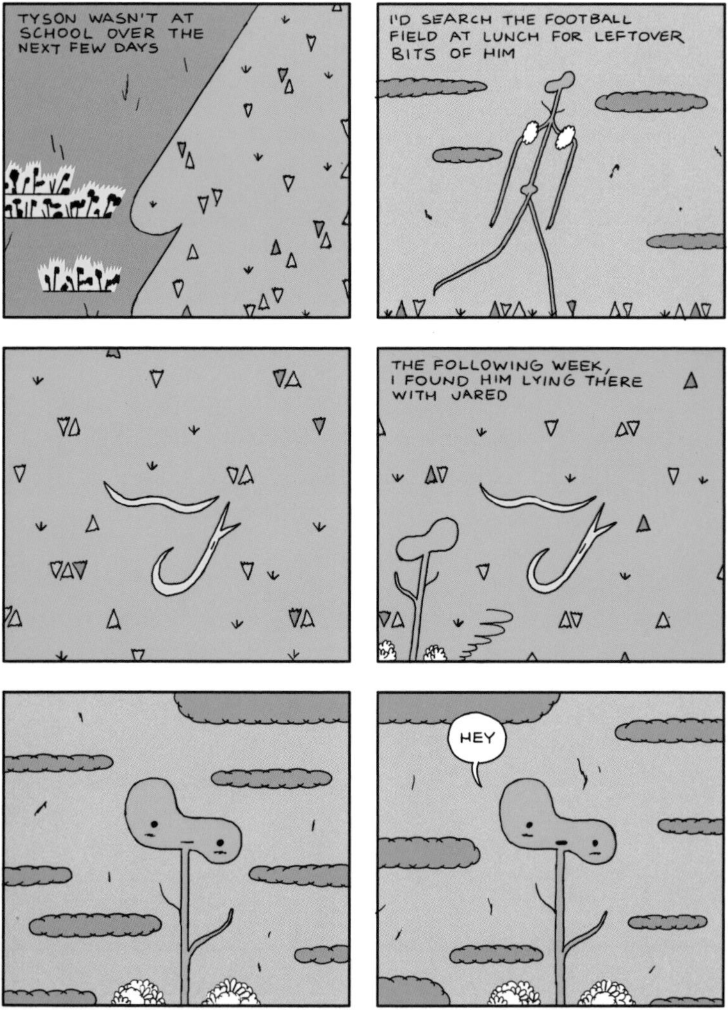
TYSON WASN'T AT SCHOOL OVER THE NEXT FEW DAYS
I'D SEARCH THE FOOTBALL FIELD AT LUNCH FOR LEFTOVER BITS OF HIM
THE FOLLOWING WEEK, I FOUND HIM LYING THERE WITH JARED
HEY

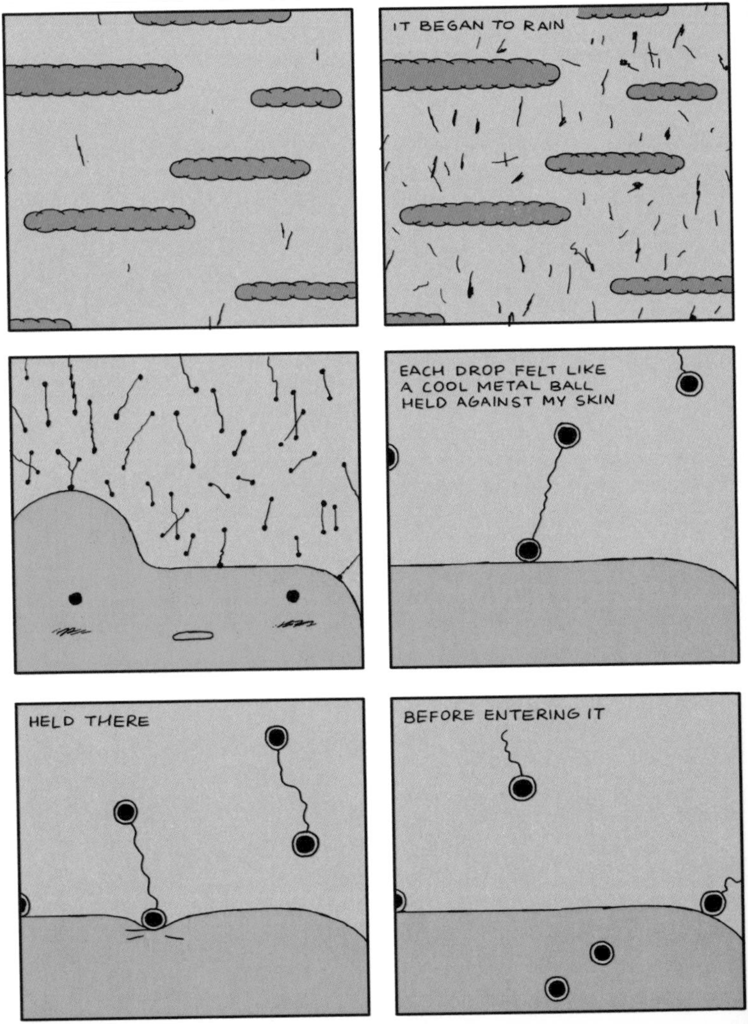

IT BEGAN TO RAIN
EACH DROP FELT LIKE A COOL METAL BALL HELD AGAINST MY SKIN
HELD THERE
BEFORE ENTERING IT

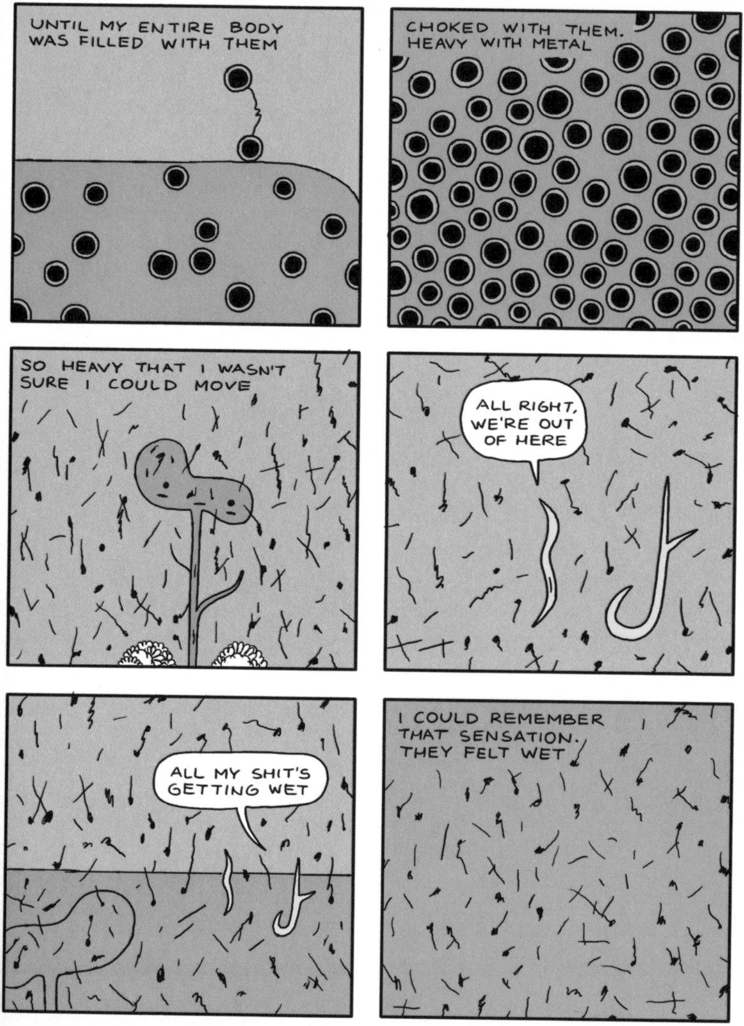
UNTIL MY ENTIRE BODY WAS FILLED WITH THEM
CHOKED WITH THEM. HEAVY WITH METAL
SO HEAVY THAT I WASN'T SURE I COULD MOVE
ALL RIGHT, WE'RE OUT OF HERE
ALL MY SHIT'S GETTING WET
I COULD REMEMBER THAT SENSATION. THEY FELT WET

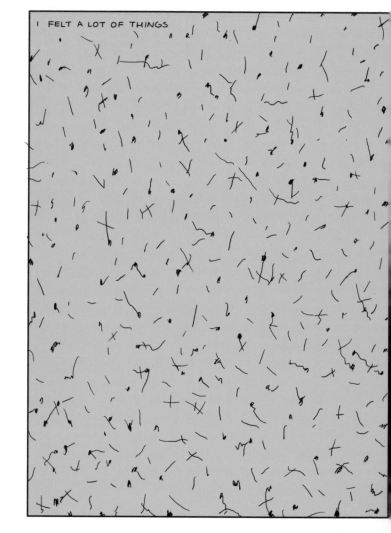
I FELT A LOT OF THINGS

THANK YOU D+Q, PATRICK, RYAN, JILLIAN, PHIL, GINETTE, ROBIN, FAMILY

DRAWNANDQUARTERLY.COM

FIRST EDITION: FEBRUARY 2016
PRINTED IN CHINA

10 9 8 7 6 5 4 3 2 1

LIBRARY AND ARCHIVES CANADA CATALOGUING IN PUBLICATION
DEFORGE, MICHAEL, 1987 – AUTHOR, ILLUSTRATOR
  BIG KIDS/MICHAEL DEFORGE.
ISBN 978-1-77046-224-3 (BOUND)
  I. GRAPHIC NOVELS. I. TITLE.
PN6733.D435B54 2016   741.5'971 C2015-904924-5

PUBLISHED IN THE USA BY DRAWN & QUARTERLY, A CLIENT PUBLISHER OF FARRAR, STRAUS AND GIROUX.
ORDERS: 888.330.8477

PUBLISHED IN CANADA BY DRAWN & QUARTERLY, A CLIENT PUBLISHER OF RAINCOAST BOOKS.
ORDERS: 888.663.5714

PUBLISHED IN THE UNITED KINGDOM BY DRAWN & QUARTERLY, A CLIENT PUBLISHER OF PUBLISHERS GROUP UK
ORDERS: INFO@PGUK.CO.UK

Canada   NOUS RECONNAISSONS L'APPUI DU GOUVERNEMENT DU CANADA/WE ACKNOWLEDGE THE SUPPORT OF THE GOVERNMENT OF CANADA AND THE CANADA COUNCIL FOR THE ARTS FOR OUR PUBLISHING PROGRAM

5-26-16

8-8-19-12-72-21

18
2

A(CHX)

2